D1241377

A PRIMER FOR BUYING AND SELLING SMALL MANUFACTURING COMPANIES

A PRIMER FOR BUYING AND SELLING SMALL MANUFACTURING COMPANIES

DOUGLAS E. KELLOGG

JOHN WILEY & SONS
New York / Chichester / Brisbane / Toronto / Singapore

Library of Congress Cataloging in Publication Data:

Kellogg, Douglas E.
    A primer for buying and selling small manufacturing companies.
    Bibliography: p.
    1. Small business—Purchasing.   2. Business enter-
prises—Purchasing.   3. Business enterprises, Sale of.
4. Factories—Purchasing.   I. Title.
HD2341.K44   1987   658.1'6   87-19017
ISBN 0-471-85235-X

To my son

Randolph Webster Kellogg

Preface

Buying or selling small business enterprises is distinctly different from starting a venture from scratch or operating an established company. Starting a business venture involves assembling a wide variety of resources and organizing and controlling them to achieve predetermined objectives. Although new entrepreneurs can tap a vast supply of advice and guidance, most new ventures today are still assembled and operated by trial and error and the majority fail before they are five years old.

Entrepreneurs who buy a going business probably expect that by doing so they will reduce their risk of failure. Entrepreneurs contemplating the sale of a successful business are primarily concerned with achieving the liquidity that would enable them to go into a new venture or to retire.

This book is designed to help entrepreneurs who wish to buy or sell control of an established manufacturing business.

Although a buyer's and a seller's interests often conflict, they ultimately have to work out all the disagreements so that a purchase and sale can take place. Having been both a buyer and seller of small manufacturing companies, I have tried to present both viewpoints as well as some elements of common knowledge and conventional wisdom that should be helpful to buyers and sellers alike.

Both owners and seekers of small manufacturing businesses should have specific goals and detailed plans to achieve these goals. The well-prepared seller will get more for his or her business than one who has not done the necessary homework. An uninformed buyer will surely get "a pig in a poke." If both buyer and seller are knowledgeable and well prepared, the risks and disappointments are minimized (but never completely eliminated) and a fair deal will result.

Regardless of what financial statements show, what an appraiser tells you, or what value you place on a business, the only true fair market value is that which is agreed on in a deal between a knowledgeable and willing buyer and a knowledgeable and willing seller acting freely and without duress or ulterior motive. However, no business activity is without a fringe of fools and frauds. Small manufacturing companies have their share.

A buyer should beware of deals that seem too good to be true, those that offer fabulous future rewards, hidden liabilities, serious stockholder friction, tax delinquencies, and so forth. Sellers must beware of vultures who offer questionable paper based on vague promises, those who offer uncertain evidence of financial responsibility, or who have no experience in the target industry.

I have looked at more than 1000 small manufacturing companies over the last 27 years. Most of these companies were owned by very satisfied entrepreneurs, well pleased with their lot in life and enthusiastic about their work to which they happily devote an inordinate amount of energy. You can get them to talk about their business at any time of the day or night. But there are some small company owners who are in trouble. These unfortunate people have had "bad luck." Things are not going well. They are overwhelmed with problems and unfulfilled hopes. They claim that they are victims of circumstance beyond their control, such as treachery of associates, poor market conditions, lack of capital, or onerous government regulations. However, Dun & Bradstreet says that most small business failures are due to management incompetence—a judgment with which I am inclined to agree. To improve your chances of success in buying or selling a business, you must sharpen your competence.

DOUGLAS E. KELLOGG

Hanover, New Hampshire
October 1987

Acknowledgments

I would like to thank all of the people who have helped make this book possible, most of whom are my good friends, business associates, customers, suppliers, teachers, and family. Especially helpful were those employees and directors with whom I worked regularly: John Fleming, James Helmuth, Raymond and Barbara Hunicke, Willard Nelson, George Peer, Calvin Thompson, Judith Young, and all of the other officers and directors of Blackstone Industries, The Ripley Company, The Lewis Corporation, The Qualitron Corporation, Multi-Metal Wire Cloth Inc., and the State National Bank of Connecticut.

Every author's family plays an important role in his or her creative activities. Mine was no exception and I greatly appreciate the support and encouragement of my wife Jo and my children Linda, Randy, Lisa, and Diane.

D.E.K.

Contents

1

Objectives for the Buyer

Ownership of a small manufacturing company is a way of life, one that is fraught with risk, full of challenge, and immensely rewarding for those who succeed. It is also a significant factor in the economic health of the United States. Small businesses (companies with fewer than 99 employees) were expected to account for 64% of the 3 million new jobs created in the United States in 1986, according to Dun's 5000 survey conducted in February 1986.

The contribution of small business to the gainful employment of Americans surely fulfills John F. Kennedy's challenge to "ask not what your country can do for you but what you can do for your country." In keeping with the highest ideals of the free enterprise system, small business owners create satisfying jobs for their fellow Americans. Let us be thankful that we are a nation of entrepreneurs.

ENJOYMENT AND SATISFACTION

Most successful entrepreneurs really enjoy managing their businesses. They go to work early and stay late; they constantly think about the business; and they will talk to anyone who will listen and occasionally listen to anyone who will talk about the challenge and fun of running a small company.

Small business owners are an independent bunch. If you have a strong desire to be your own boss, to be totally responsible for your own welfare, to get a chance to take high risks for high rewards, then a small business is a good place to start.

Another personal advantage of being your own boss is that you never have to go through an identity crisis, which is such a popular fraud these days. Small business owners know who they are, what they are doing, and where they're going. There are no aimless or shiftless entrepreneurs.

INVESTMENT

A successful small manufacturing company can be an excellent investment for the owner/manager or for any investor who has the experience and desire to be involved in such an enterprise. For the owner/manager, the investment probably represents the bulk of his or her net worth and borrowing ability. With success, the investment certainly ought to produce a much greater yield than publicly traded securities, certificates of deposit, or other conventional investments. And the fluctuation in value of small, privately held manufacturing companies almost never follows the short-term trends in the public securities market. It follows the creative and entrepreneurial abilities of the owner.

Liquidity in a small business is manageable by the prudent owner although too much unplanned liquidity can bring an unwelcome letter from the Internal Revenue Service.

TAX ADVANTAGES

Many people do not realize that most corporate expenses (including the owner's salary and bonus) are deductible from income. In the case of S corporations, profits pass through the corporation to the owners for tax purposes. And several items of corporate expense do not involve any cash payments (e.g., depreciation).

There are also generous allowances in the form of tax credits for research and development, purchasing of certain types of assets, locating in high-unemployment areas, using disadvantaged workers, and so on.

It is quite advantageous for a high-tax bracket individual to be an active or passive owner of a small manufacturing business. Not only can the individual secure tax benefits, he or she can also enjoy many of the benefits of life insurance, deferred compensation, stock options, health and accident insurance, and even retirement benefits available to employees and directors. Congress is constantly changing the tax advantages of these benefits, but they will always be better and cheaper than nongroup benefits.

Separate ownership of certain assets (land, buildings, vehicles, machinery) by owners of the corporation can also produce valuable tax benefits. Building rents can be adjusted to inflation, depreciation is deductible against personal income, and market values of good buildings in prime areas seldom decline.

IMPROVING EXISTING BUSINESS

Owners of successful, small manufacturing companies can acquire other small manufacturing companies or product lines of larger companies. This is the route we took. Our company started out with annual sales of about $300,000. We acquired seven other small manufacturing companies or product lines (all with easily borrowed bank money), which enabled us to increase our sales steadily and profitably to over $8 million annually during a 25-year period. The strategy of our acquisition program was not only to increase our sales but to diversify our markets.

One of the special advantages of small companies acquiring other small companies is that the negotiations are conducted between two entrepreneurs who have a lot in common and a certain amount of mutual admiration. The seller is often so emotionally involved that he or she is irrationally prejudiced against many types of prospective buyers. The seller may think that buyers are not sufficiently experienced to run the company successfully or they are not credit worthy, or that the company will lose its identity, or that faithful employees will not be treated fairly. However, when the seller talks to another successful entrepreneur, such fears often fade away.

By the same token the buyer may see management practices that he or she thinks can be improved. If there are enough obvious deficiencies in the seller's management of the company, the buyer's enthusiasm increases and his or her apprehension decreases. In this way both parties become willing, even eager to make a deal.

In addition to diversifying an existing business by buying another company, a small company owner can often significantly improve the existing business. The most obvious advantage, if it is done right, is the saving of the cost of a management team. Of course, such a benefit only occurs if the business that is bought can be easily integrated with the present business, and can be run more effectively under one roof with a single team of managers.

Your first question may be, how can I run a second business when I am already up to my ears in my first business? The answer is that you use your own talents and those of your employees more effectively (see the section "Training" in Chapter 9).

We run five acquired companies with one management team. We have good division managers (formerly department foremen) and we keep only the best workers of the acquired companies. True, we had to add a few staff people such as a controller, an export manager (when export sales got up to $1 million), and an advertising manager. Some of these functions may start out as part-time jobs for line managers. The company hires specialists for this work only when sales volume justifies it.

In every acquisition we made, we have been able to reduce overhead costs (sometimes direct costs too, with our economy of increased size) and, at the same time, we increased sales of the new acquisitions through our well-established distribution system. If you have good people whom you respect and trust, give them as much responsibility as they can handle, and pick good acquisitions, you can add very profitable volume to your existing business. (Further discussion of corporate acquisition programs appears in Chapter 9.)

GOOD INCOME

For the enthusiastic and successful full-time owner/manager, a handsome salary, steady increases in personal net worth, and many other perfectly honest benefits are all available as rewards of the entrepreneur. In 1984 the average compensation (salary and bonus) of chief executive officers in 46 small manufacturing companies with annual sales under $10 million was $110,000 per year. Average after-tax profit of the companies in this survey was $246,000.[*]

If you want to consider the avoidance of expense (like the avoidance of taxes) as income, a small manufacturing company is an ideal vehicle for personal expense avoidance (company car, health and life insurance, savings or pension program, free turkeys, discount on company-made or -purchased products, etc.). The federal government is constantly trying to reduce this private welfare in favor of more public welfare, but small business owners are a very clever breed and will always be one jump ahead of the bureaucrats.

PROFITABLE SPECULATION

A small manufacturing company can be a great speculative investment for a private investor—better than a lot of publicly traded companies, much better than many REITs (real estate investment trusts), oil exploration ventures, certainly better than WPPSS (Washington Public Power Supply System bonds which are in default, often irreverently referred to as "WHOOPS" bonds). On one hand, successful small business owners seldom go looking for secondary

_____

[*]Executive Compensation Service Inc., Fort Lee, N.J.

equity outside of friends and family. But on the other, entrepreneurs do grow old and tired and some do not have children or other relatives who are interested in carrying on the business (they want the cash).

Occasionally, these owners have business acquaintances or friends whom they may turn to for advice and counsel when the day approaches for retirement. Being a respected friend of a small business owner whose heirs are uninterested in the business can be mutually rewarding. How do you find such opportunities? Join the small business groups, go to their seminars, talk to your banker and accountant about your interest in investing in small business.

Chapter 12, which discusses "leveraged liquidity," clearly shows a place for outside investors in small companies. All you need is $50,000 or $100,000 to buy yourself a substantial piece of a small company.

DIVERSIFICATION OF ASSETS

After many years of hard work and sacrifice, you find yourself the debt-free owner of a company that makes vacuum tubes for radios. You can see that the market for these tubes is rapidly being taken over by semiconductors. One option is to close the doors and auction off the assets. Or you can go out and put your assets to work in an acquisition that will ease you painlessly out of the dying vacuum tube business.

You may instead have a successful company making a seasonal or regional product and you would like to diversify your sales into other counter or nonseasonal or nonregional products. Or you would like to increase your average order value with synergistic products.

You can base the choice to diversify on several factors:

1. *The Need To Be More Profitable.* You have too much overhead for your volume and you can not figure out how to increase your volume without increasing overhead.

2. *The Need To Use Existing Resources More Effectively.* Your machinery, buildings, or managers are not being used to their fullest capacity.

3. *Economic Cycles.* You would like to have products that sell well in all kinds of economic conditions. Do-it-yourself products generally do well in recessions. Luxury consumer goods sell well in good times. Sales of industrial equipment and supplies follow the economic welfare of major industries. The pulp and paper industry might be up when basic metals are down.

4. *Geographic Diversity.* It is nice to have customers in every major population area in the market. If sales in the rust belt decline, they might be better in the sun belt or west coast or New England. If you have a consumer product, your rural customers may react to a different economic tune than your urban customers. We like to sell in every major population area in every state in the United States. We therefore look for acquisitions that have sales or potential sales in all geographic areas. It's not only a safety factor, it's good business.

5. *Export.* To many small manufacturers export business is considered either bonus business (because it often carries no marketing overhead) or a nuisance because of the difficult paperwork, communications and language problems, packaging and shipping requirements, extended payment terms if you grant credit, and foreign electrical requirements if you have an electrical product. However, many small companies have direct or indirect export sales of 10 or 20% of total sales.

It is to the advantage of the United States to develop more export sales and both state and federal governments are encouraging small business to pursue foreign trade. Within the next decade the United States has to become more aggressive in world trade and this emphasis will certainly filter down to smaller companies.

INDEPENDENCE

One of the most compelling reasons to own a small manufacturing business is the strong sense of independence that comes only from ownership. You are the captain of your own ship (but you may also be the galley slave if you're not careful).

There are many nonmanufacturing businesses for sale. Their sales may be greater than those of a manufacturing business of comparable net worth and they may be acquired for less money. Why, then, is a manufacturing business more desirable and why does it offer more independence? Here are a few reasons:

1. A manufacturing business has greater control over its own destiny. It designs, fabricates, and sells its own product. It controls costs and generates earnings on three levels (design, production, and marketing).

2. In many cases the location of a manufacturing business is not important to success, especially if it has national or international sales. This is often a deciding factor for the owner to whom location has great personal importance.

3. A small manufacturing company is extremely versatile. It can quickly change its policies, products, and personnel

to fit rapidly changing circumstances. It can take advantage of unexpected opportunities.

The independence of the owner of a small manufacturing business depends on his or her ability to find good managers, train and lead them well, reward them fairly, and ultimately delegate all responsibilities except the most critical strategic decisions.

Your objectives in acquiring a small manufacturing company should be established as flexible priorities because otherwise you could miss opportunities that you might otherwise find acceptable. If you have your heart set on an industrial plastics manufacturing business and a good deal comes along on a company making metal stampings, you might consider starting off in metal stampings and acquiring a plastics division later on. Don't let the product dominate your objectives.

By the same token don't sacrifice earning power for the sake of having the product you want. Although much satisfaction lies in being in the industry or product line you like, all small manufacturing companies have similar management challenges and can offer learning and experience value if nothing else.

Be prepared to modify your objectives as you progress in your search for the perfect opportunity.

ALTERNATIVE TARGETS

Many seekers of small manufacturing companies are disappointed after months of searching, dozens of interviews, and no attractive opportunities. Before you spend six months or a year trying to find your ideal acquisition, develop some alternatives that can ultimately lead you to your primary goal and provide valuable experience and training in the meantime.

If you can't find the company you want in your targeted industry, look at suppliers to the industry. For example, look for a machine shop that sells $1 million worth of machined parts to this industry. Many of these vendors are small companies serving relatively few local customers and are often owned and operated by machinists who have worked in your targeted industry. There are about 35,000 machine shops in the United States listed in many different directories of manufacturing companies (e.g., 6319 in California, 2672 in Texas, 2026 in Ohio, etc.) and at any given time there are probably 7500 of them for sale. Names and addresses of these companies are available from chambers of commerce in almost any area in which you want to locate.

The price of a machine shop is frequently not much more than the value of the machinery plus land and building (if included). Your first acquisition could be such a shop with 12 customers, some of whom might be desirable acquisition prospects for you. If you took this route you would have your foot in the door with some valuable management experience, a going concern, some skilled employees, and a cash flow that you can use to convince your bank to finance the acquisition of another company.

A machine shop could provide helpful experience in the manufacture of parts for subsequent acquisitions. It also presents an opportunity to sharpen up your marketing skills. And best of all, it opens up lots of doors to other potential acquisitions. Our first acquisition was a machine shop making parts for a major aircraft manufacturer. After our second acquisition (a machinery manufacturer) two years later we sold the machine shop.

There are other suppliers to industry who enjoy "niche"

businesses furnishing all types of goods and services. Some examples would be manufacturers of filter cloth, high-purity gas valves, cabinets and cases, special saw blades, thermocouple wire, railroad ties, hinges, and special purpose motors. Now is a good time to establish your objectives, outline a course of action to achieve these objectives, set some time limits, and get going.

2

Objectives for the Seller

Many owners of small manufacturing companies do not like to think about selling their business and thus simply decide never to retire. I have talked to dozens of owners who are in their 70s and 80s who have no idea of retiring and only a vague idea of what might happen when they become unable to manage their business. One result of this attitude is the growing number of manufacturing businesses owned and operated by bereaved spouses, most of whom would rather be doing something else.

Those owners who have children interested in the business generally relinquish management to them, but the failure rate among second or third generation owners is surprisingly high. Furthermore, dissent among owners is more prevalent among family-owned businesses.

It is probably more important for sellers to have carefully structured plans of disposition than it is for buyers to have acquisition plans. Buyers can develop their strategy as they carry on their search for the ideal acquisition, but the seller without a plan can't attract good prospects and can be victimized by an unscrupulous buyer. Without a plan, the seller may be at the mercy of an aggressive buyer who will make one for him or her (see Chapter 4).

ESTABLISHING FAIR MARKET VALUE

There are several standard procedures for establishing the fair market value of a business. The most common is probably a formal appraisal of the business by an independent business appraiser. The appraisal offers valuable comparisons with other similar situations, multiple of earnings ratios for an industry, specific asset valuations, and assessments of the general economic climate in which the seller proposes to sell the business. A buyer needs this kind of information. If the seller can't supply a recent appraisal of the business, the buyer may have an independent appraisal made by his or her own appraiser.

A preliminary estimate of the value of the business can be done quickly by the owner. Take the average of the last five years' earnings before tax and multiply it by five. This may or may not indicate an acceptable value. Five times earnings is a commonly used multiple for valuing small manufacturing companies that are not in high-technology or specialized industries.

If five times earnings does not produce a reasonable fair market value, earnings can be adjusted for unusual expenses or costs. An accountant can help to identify such items: wages and salaries that are out-of-line, unusual travel, entertainment and selling expenses, nonrecurring losses, abnormal fluctuations in sales, unfavorable inventory levels, or turnover. The buyer is going to go through this exercise so the seller would be well advised to make his or her own calculations in order to anticipate any adjustments the buyer may make.

If no amount of figuring produces a plausible price-earnings ratio, then the owner has to correct the situation (see Chapter 5) or value the business on a different basis.

Another method for estimating fair market value if there are no significant earnings is to emphasize the value of the assets. If a company has a strong balance sheet and no earnings, making the company profitable may not be difficult. The seller's challenge then is to persuade the buyer how easy it would be to turn the company around.

Some small high-technology companies with losses are valued in terms of annual sales. Fair market values may be estimated at one or two times annual sales. This is a blue-sky method of valuation with the buyer assuming the risk of generating a profit where none has been shown.

A seller should remember that losses carried forward (or current) could be an attractive advantage to a corporate buyer in the top tax bracket. Or, by the same token, a seller's high tax earnings can also be an advantage to a buyer with losses and paying no taxes.

In the final analysis, the fair market value placed on a seller's business has to be based on real demonstrable value; and the more convincing the demonstration of that value is, the more likely the seller will get a decent price.

FINDING A BUYER

A seller has a much more difficult challenge in finding a suitable buyer than a buyer has in finding an attractive manufacturing business. This might seem paradoxical when there are so many more buyers than there are sellers, but the problem lies in the lack of a clearly identifiable market place or marketing mechanism for the buying and selling of small manufacturing companies. It is true that there are thousands of business brokers who have lists of companies for sale and these lists (or individual items from these lists) are widely circulated, but many deals made in this unstructured market do not work out. Why? Because the buyer and the seller are not well matched.

This random nature of the market means the buyer must look at about 100 opportunities to find one that is a good match. In talking with some principals in unsuccessful deals with small companies, we have observed a direct correlation between the number of prospects considered by the buyer and the success of the acquisition. If you look at three opportunities before you buy, your chance of success is less than when you look at 50 or 100 opportunities.

Using this ratio in reverse would seem to suggest that a seller must be prepared to talk to 50 to 100 prospective buyers, especially if the buyer is sharing the risk in financing the deal. With a brokerage, 100 buyer prospects can be located quickly but many would be unqualified. We recommend that the seller first try to preselect prospects through a trusted third party (probably the company lawyers or accountants).

Because the sale of a business can be very upsetting to communities, employees, customers, and suppliers it is best to keep the planning and negotiating confidential.

Any well-established small manufacturing company with annual sales over $1 million is likely to be on many mailing lists of brokers and acquisition consultants, who send out letters stating that they represent a well-known company looking for acquisitions and that your company seems to meet their requirements. They will also ask you to call them and will tell you that there is no obligation or charge as they are paid by their client. (We receive as many as five of these letters per month.)

How do these brokers and consultants get a company's name? It's easy—they look at product directories such as Thomas Register and at advertising and news releases in appropriate trade papers. They send for catalogs, they buy mailing lists, they even order Dun & Bradstreet reports.

Prospects for buying a company fall into several categories: directly and indirectly related, and directly and indirectly contacted. We recommend that the buyer search these categories in order:

Directly Related Prospects

Obvious prospects for buying your company include customers, suppliers, competitors, personally known business associates (including owners of other companies), and companies or individuals who have approached you directly (not through brokers or other third parties).

You may have some ideas about prospects that don't fit this category. Let's say that you're a small manufacturer of specialized hand tools and you like the idea of selling your company to Stanley, Cooper, or Disston. Without too much trouble you can arrange to meet personally with a senior officer in any of these companies, who can steer you through the right channels to get serious and confidential consideration.

Look closely at your 10 largest customers. The chances are that they are larger companies than yours. They may even be from the "Fortune 500" (which would probably not be good prospects) or better yet, successful smaller companies anxious to expand by acquisition.

Any expansion-minded company looks at some of its customers as acquisition prospects. You are the customer of your suppliers. Look at the 10 largest ones as prospective buyers of your company.

Seldom in the world of small manufacturing companies are there antitrust or restraint of trade problems. Therefore your most formidable competitors are good prospects for acquiring your company. But beware of competitors who say they are interested but who actually are interested only in seeing your financial statements, picking your brains, and filching your clever ideas. The advantages of merging with small competitors are especially attractive for the dominant company.

Business acquaintances from trade associations, chambers of commerce, and social activities can all be rich sources of buyer prospects. If a successful friend knows your company and has told you he would like to buy it if you ever decided to sell, he may well be an excellent prospect. In trade association seminars and industry conferences you will always meet successful owners or managers of other companies.

As previously indicated, you have probably received many inquiries directly from other companies or investors who have stated that they are interested in acquiring your company. If you have told them that you did not wish to sell your company yet but would contact them if conditions changed, you might review these inquiries, pick out some and set up an appointment to talk.

As you will note, pursuing directly related prospects does not involve significant cost other than your time.

Indirectly Related Prospects

At the same time you are seeking directly related prospects, you should start looking at indirectly related prospects which include your board of directors, your bank, attorneys, accountants, and consultants (who are qualified and who have worked for you). All of these sources of prospects have a vested interest in your company. You pay them for their services and most of them know you and your company quite well. Most of them would like to continue their relationship with the new owners of your company. Therefore they will look diligently for buyers among their clients. The author's company has found this to be an excellent source of buyer as well as seller prospects. We have acquired one company and sold one as a direct result of suggestions by our professional advisors.

One other source of indirectly related prospects is the individual "finder." This professional person has developed a lot of business contacts and knows "what's going on" in the areas of your interest. Reliable "finders" are rare but they can be sources of good prospects if you are lucky enough to find a good one. Compensation is negotiable but there is some risk of losing confidentiality.

Direct Contacts

With directly and indirectly related prospects no advertising or publicity is involved. All contacts with prospects are private and confidential, although some information regarding your intentions will inevitably leak out if a serious prospect is not forthcoming within a few months.

However, direct contacts include advertising, or direct contact with prospects personally, by mail or phone. A classified ad in *The Wall Street Journal* or other trade publication will bring a wide variety of inquiries, many of which will be from brokers, agents, finders, and curious individuals (possibly including employees or competitors). If you can arrange to have all inquiries sent to your lawyers or accountants, you can remain anonymous and pick and choose the inquiries you wish to follow up.

Direct mail can be used with a mailing list of prospects you have put together from your own records: companies that have contacted you, companies that you would like to talk to, and private investors.

Personal contact with carefully chosen prospects can be productive and informative especially if you have a compelling advantage to present to the prospect, such as a proposal to increase the prospect's profitability greatly or to provide some desirable tax advantages. Most entrepreneurs welcome the opportunity to discuss such matters. This should, of course, be done on an owner-to-owner basis, in confidence.

Indirect Contacts

Indirect contacts are business brokers and consultants, who work under a contract to receive a substantial commission if a deal closes. This commission is always agreed upon in advance and often has a long tail (sometimes more than one year).

Like a real estate listing, the arrangement can be exclusive or nonexclusive. Brokers fees are generally negotiable although many use formulas like this on gross sales price (specifically defined to fit the transaction):

Sales price of less than $1,000,000
First $500,000 or portion thereof—10%
Next $500,000 or portion thereof—6%

Sales price of more than $1,000,000
First $1,000,000—5%
Second $1,000,000 or portion thereof—4%
Third $1,000,000 or portion thereof—3%
Fourth $1,000,000 or portion thereof—2%
Fifth $1,000,000 or portion thereof—1%

Although we have solicited lists from many brokers (for acquisition prospects) all over the United States and Canada and receive as many as three or four lists or single prospects per month, we have succeeded in buying only one company listed by a broker in 20 years. In all fairness to brokers it must be said that they have produced a lot of good acquisition prospects for us and we have spent much time in visiting and negotiating with these prospects and we continue to do so. Many brokers offer valuable services and earn every penny of their commissions in active and knowledgeable participation in the negotiations.

Merger consultants who are retained by larger companies (most often to search for acquisitions) are skilled in locating prospects and in preparing a comprehensive prospectus on the acquisition for their client. Although these consultants may claim that they have a client specifically interested in your company or that your company is exactly what they are looking for, they are frequently just fishing for listings, which they then peddle to several clients. However, in many cases these consultants will agree to reveal the name of their client to you if you will simply indicate your interest in a preliminary discussion. In these cases the client has agreed to pay the consultant's fee so you really have nothing to lose.

Advice to the seller is almost the same as to the buyer: Now is a good time to establish your objectives, prepare a good prospectus on your company, outline a course of action to achieve your objectives, set some time limits, and get going.

For the seller who cannot find a suitable buyer or get a reasonable offer for a business, a restructuring of the business might be the only alternative except liquidation. Chapter 5 discusses this alternative.

3

What Are Your Resources?

In all of life's endeavors an individual's success or failure depends to a great extent on his or her ability to understand, to analyze and solve problems, and to recognize opportunities. Good or bad luck is often credited with causing success or failure, but it is seldom a major factor.

WHAT ARE YOUR OWN RESOURCES?

The most important aspect of your own resources is an overwhelming desire to "be in charge," to be the boss, to direct the activities of others, and to make things happen. But you must be qualified before you can be in charge of anything. You need knowledge and some experience. You must be a quick learner and you must have ideas. You've got to have leadership qualities and be able to influence other people. You must be meticulously honest with yourself and others. Success in business is measured in the level of satisfaction of investors, employees, suppliers, and customers.

Investors want a fair return on their money. Some expect more, others expect less. The successful entrepreneurs satisfy the majority.

Employees want fair treatment in the work place. They also want an interesting challenge to match their talents. They will work productively and happily under imaginative leadership.

Suppliers want to be paid promptly. They don't want to be constantly irritated by unreasonable demands and whimsical changes. The well-organized, considerate, dependable entrepreneur is one who gets good service from suppliers.

Customers want good value, honestly offered and reasonably serviced. All manufacturing and service industries have some customers who seem to be impossible to please. Again the entrepreneur must do his or her best to satisfy the majority. The successful entrepreneur acquires a reputation of excellent, if not outstanding customer service and strives to exceed more often than falling short of the expectations of others.

DO YOUR TALENTS FIT THE OPPORTUNITY?

If you are starting a company from scratch, your personal interests will lead you to opportunities that you think you will enjoy. There may be interesting products, people, locations, or a challenging problem that must be solved. Regardless of the character of the opportunity, however, you should assess the value of your personal contribution to the target enterprise.

Similarly, if you are buying into an existing business you should have some idea of what your impact will be as a member, if not the leader of the organization. Most buyers of controlling interests in small businesses fully expect to exert considerable influence on the business. Their personalities and ideas will shape the future of the business for better or worse or, in some cases, produce no effect whatsoever.

Your talents and experience will be perceived by the employees, stockholders, and customers as potentially beneficial, detrimental, or ineffective. It's up to you to sell the beneficial aspects of whatever you bring to the enterprise.

WHAT IS YOUR EARNING POWER?

Some seekers of small manufacturing companies have a good record of earnings in other businesses and can set a realistic goal on their earning ability. In many cases a person considers buying a business for the sole purpose of increasing personal income. In other cases potential entrepreneurs cannot find happiness or satisfaction in working for anyone else and are forced to go into business for themselves regardless of the income potential.

Whatever your motivation and apparent earning power, you should realize that your earnings as the sole owner and chief executive of a small manufacturing company depend entirely on the success of your leadership. If you are buying a going business, you can quickly determine the compensation of the chief executive seller. You should also be able to figure out if this can be enhanced under your ownership.

Owners' salaries and benefits vary tremendously in small companies. Very profitable operations can yield high salaries. I have analyzed acquisition prospects where the owner was receiving a salary of $150,000 per year from a business with annual sales of $500,000. I have seen other companies where the owner had to be satisfied with $15,000 per year on sales of $1 million because he wasn't able to control the enterprise properly.

For a well-established, growing manufacturing business with a 10% pre-tax profit margin, the chief executive (and sole owner) should receive compensation of at least $10,000 per year for every $100,000 of sales up to $1 million and performance bonuses for sales over $1 million.

WHAT ARE YOUR ASSETS DOING FOR YOU NOW?

A quick analysis of your current personal net worth will tell you what your assets are earning or costing now. Any owner or prospective owner of a business should be thoroughly familiar with the process for determining and understanding net worth and fair market value.

Simply stated, net worth is assets minus liabilities: the bottom line of the balance sheet. For a personal balance sheet the following items are generally considered to be important:

Assets. Cash in banks, certificates of deposit, time deposits, money market funds, and so on; investments such as precious metals, stocks (including equity in your own company), bonds, income-producing real estate, interest-bearing loans (to your company or others); real estate (nonincome producing) such as primary residence, vacation homes, unimproved land; and readily salable personal property such as aircraft, boats, recreational vehicles, autos, and so on.

Liabilities. Personal loans, mortgage loans, other secured obligations (life insurance loans, and so on), amounts due on credit purchases, accounts payable.

Net Worth. Assets minus liabilities.

You should have records so that you can list some assets at cost (plus capital improvements). Items such as residences, land, and collectibles purchased many years ago are often undervalued when listed at cost (unless they have deteriorated substantially from fair or unfair wear and tear or have lost their value due to other reasons). Net worth should be figured two ways using both the cost value and current fair market value. The spread is a measure of your competence as an investor and manager.

If you have a significant net worth (over $100,000) made up of marketable securities or other liquid assets, your financial management ability will be reflected in the earnings (or increase in fair market value) of these assets. This factor is important as an index not only of your managerial skills but also of your credit worthiness: You are the sort of person who would probably be successful as a business owner if you manage your personal finances efficiently. Lenders look for such signs of reliability.

Determine what your assets are doing for you now and what they might do if some were invested in a small manufacturing business.

WHAT IS YOUR BORROWING POWER?

Recent years have seen substantial activity in "leveraged buyouts:" a deal where a lender puts up most of the money and is paid back out of earnings of the leveraged asset.

Often a successful business owner will sell on generous terms if he or she has complete confidence in the buyer's ability to generate enough profit to pay back the obligation.

Nevertheless, you will seldom find a deal where the down payment is zero: You have to come up with a reasonable initial payment. Again, it is not conventional to borrow all of the initial payment. Lenders do not like a situation where the buyer takes no personal risk at all.

If the assets of the sale are well worth the purchase price (i.e., easily converted into cash such as current and balanced inventories, good accounts receivable, excellent machinery easily liquidated, and good real estate), then the lender might loan 90% of the purchase price with the buyer putting up 10%.

In this case you have to put up $50,000 when you go to the lender. Your borrowing power is $450,000 when you negotiate to buy $500,000 worth of good assets.

These same ratios can apply to deals up to several million dollars. If you can't manage the down payment yourself, you'll have to consider some partners.

HOW MUCH TIME ARE YOU WILLING TO DEVOTE?

If you are going to sell your business, you must allocate a substantial part of your time to preparing the business for sale. Not only do you have to get your financial statements looking good to a prospective buyer, but you may have to make changes in your manufacturing or administration to effect these changes. It could take a long time, months or perhaps several years.

You must develop a plan with the help of your accountant and lawyer. You must put a realistic fair market value on the business, make a list of prospective buyers and plan your selling strategy.

If you have delegated as much responsibility as possible to your trusted employees, you should be able to find time to do a careful and thorough job of preparing your business for sale.

If you are trying to purchase a business and juggle a full-time job, you will, of course, have to devote nights, weekends, and vacations to your search and analysis duties. But, as a true entrepreneur, you enjoy this type of activity so much that you have probably been thinking about it most of your adult life. All you really need is more opportunities to look at.

Most entrepreneurs started their careers working for someone else, realizing at an early stage that they had to be their own boss. It is not difficult to acquire a business by working at it in your spare time. Your duties consist mostly of search, analysis, and inspection of likely prospects. When you get to the point where some money has to change hands, you will have determined what your income will be in the acquired business and you can then notify your employer of your new job.

Being a buyer is much easier than being a seller.

CREATIVE IMAGINATION

One of the principal attributes of successful entrepreneurs is a creative imagination. They must see things that others don't see. They must be able to understand and simplify complex relationships and difficult problems. And they need the experience or intuition (preferably both) to analyze an opportunity quickly and accurately.

My old Army Staff Officers Field Manual FM101-5, dated July 1940, and prepared by unnamed and unknown authors, states that a commander must make an estimate of the situation and to do this he needs the essential elements of information. This process is second nature to true entrepreneurs—they know instinctively how to size up a business situation and they know how to use their trusted servants, What, Who, When, Where, How, and Why.

There is no authority that says that an entrepreneur has to have a creative imagination, but it is obvious that creativity is an essential element in the success of the entrepreneur. In the 1950s Alex Osborn of BBDO popularized the idea of "brainstorming," which is applying creative thinking to the solution of business problems. Also, in 1955, a student research group at the Harvard Business School published a critical study of techniques and programs for stimulating creative thinking in business called "Imagination—Undeveloped Resource."

Although the term *brainstorming* has faded from use, the idea of the creative leader has become more important with the constantly increasing complexity of businesses. The computer in business today has spawned new concepts like MIS (Management Information Systems), MRP (Material Requirements Planning), and a host of other management control techniques. These are new tools with which the entrepreneur must be familiar. Creative imagination is more important today than it has ever been in the past and entrepreneurs are proving it.

LEADERSHIP

More is written about industrial leadership than any other management quality, probably because it's the most elusive quality of management. The successful entrepreneur has to be a good leader. Without this skill he will most surely fail.

Leadership in its simplest form might be defined as knowing what has to be done and getting other people to do it enthusiastically.

As a director of several small manufacturing companies, I have the interesting and valuable opportunity to observe chief executives at work. Some of them appear to be excellent leaders; others do not. Some have a high rate of success in making management decisions, although most would probably agree that at least 25% of their decisions were not ideal. Some have made horrendous mistakes that have resulted in terminal business failures and great personal anguish. One of the elements of failure seems to be random activity toward indefinite goals. Good leadership avoids this problem.

The measurement of leadership quality is not only reflected in the profit and loss statement and the increase in stockholder equity; it is most apparent in the quality of the enterprise and the efficiency of the organization. The scale of measurement is different for different people.

HOW TO GET STARTED

This is the process by which you determine what to do. If you are an experienced and knowledgeable buyer, seller, or operator of business enterprises, you have undoubtedly developed a system to find and analyze opportunities and to solve business problems successfully. You are probably also blessed with an intuitive sense of being able to recognize winners and losers earlier than other people. But if you are on the outer perimeter of the entrepreneurial world and just beginning to acquire a taste for adventure in buying, selling, and operating small business ventures, then you are looking for the magic formula that tells you how to be successful. Unfortunately there is no magic formula. But there is a growing body of conventional wisdom of entrepreneurism that bears reviewing.

SITUATION ANALYSIS

As a new buyer, seller, or operator, you have your plate full of opportunities and problems. You have to recognize them, sort them out, analyze them, and develop a plan of action.

The analysis of a problem or opportunity is what is called in military parlance an "estimate of the situation," which follows a very precise program of looking at every factor in the situation and extracting the essential elements of information. By this process you gather information and study the circumstances leading up to the situation, look carefully at the present state of affairs, and then determine how things might work out in the future. If you are the prime mover in the situation, you then have to see that a plan is developed (see Chapters 4 and 5) to achieve the objectives that have been established.

This idea sounds ridiculously simple but, in fact, it is incredibly difficult and there are many losers and few winners.

INTUITIVE SKILLS

Successful entrepreneurs seem to have intuitive skills that make things look easy. Can these skills be developed by a person of ordinary ability and undistinguished accomplishments? Perhaps.

The key to acquiring these skills is learning through direct personal experience. You've got to have a burning desire and deep personal involvement. If your goal is to buy an existing company, you must go through the entire process of learning how to find a company, how to determine values, how to negotiate the purchase, how to operate the company, and ultimately how to sell or trade it.

Success requires fast and accurate learning ability, creative ways to solve problems and recognize opportunities, and leadership skills. Once you have acquired and practiced these attributes of success, they seem to sink into the subconscious and become "intuitive" but they are really learned skills.

Interpersonal abilities (leadership) are especially important because an entrepreneur spends much of his or her time trying to influence other people.

Most entrepreneurs I have known are not self-seeking zealots whose only goals are wealth, personal power, and influence. The successful entrepreneurs tend to feel a strong social obligation to be an independent force for creating and developing new ideas in products and services as well as jobs, work efficiency, social and economic improvements, and other good causes.

Of course, it also takes entrepreneurial skills to print your own money, develop Ponzi swindles (named after a swindler, these are swindles or schemes that are fraudulent offerings to the public of very high return investments in which a few early investors (swindlers) are paid the high returns out of money paid in by later investors. No returns are paid to actual investors and the swindlers disappear with the money.) or steal cars but these activities carry unacceptably high risks and a very low moral status and cannot possibly result in any real, lasting satisfaction to the sincere entrepreneur.

The challenge of being an entrepreneur is well worth the risks and the stress. Try it. You'll like it.

4

Planning
for the Buyer

With all of the unavoidable risks of buying manufacturing companies, try to minimize these risks with a carefully constructed plan. Furthermore, if you will need financing, you can't go to a lender without a detailed plan.

A business plan is an essential element in buying or selling a manufacturing enterprise. It is a virtual requirement whether the lender is a bank, venture capitalist, SBIC (Small Business Investment Corporation), or private investor. It is also the basis for analysis for the buyer or the seller.

If a business plan could be completely objective and totally factual, it would serve all interested parties equally well. Buyers, sellers, and lenders, however, have different interests and will analyze the opportunity from a different perspective.

The seller wants to present the company in the best possible way to achieve a good price and terms. The buyer probably has different concepts of value and may want to "redeploy" the assets according to his or her ideas of how the company can yield the best results. The lender wants to be sure that the loan can be repaid on schedule, and the equity investor wants to be assured of growth and/or income from the investment.

These are often conflicting objectives and a final agreement can be reached only by careful analysis and can easily go wrong because of incorrect or incomplete information, erroneous assumptions, as well as forecasts and projections that are too conservative or too optimistic.

Very few buyers or sellers of small companies bother to prepare a business plan for the purchase or sale of the target company. If no plan is prepared by either party, both parties enter negotiations poorly informed. The buyer is probably at the greater disadvantage.

HOW TO WRITE A BUSINESS PLAN

There are as many ways to write a business plan as there are buyers. The best plan is one that will help close the deal.

A typical plan covers a summary of the situation with the buyer's objective clearly stated. The target company must be described and analyzed in detail. An acceptable description of the target company might follow this outline:

DESCRIPTION OF THE TARGET COMPANY

A. General
   1. History of target company
   2. Corporate structure

3. List of officers and directors
4. Stockholders
5. Organization chart
   a. Key managers
   b. Total number of employees
6. Management philosophy
   a. General
   b. Growth pattern
   c. Labor relations
   d. R&D activities (innovation)
7. Strengths and weaknesses
   a. Marketing skills
   b. Manufacturing skills
   c. Administration and planning skills
   d. Financial skills
8. Legal and accounting
9. Consultants
10. Public relations
11. Patents, trademarks and copyrights

B. Financial
   1. Profit and loss statements or extracts for 5 to 10 years
   2. Balance sheets for 5 to 10 years
   3. Ratios
   4. Estimates of current operations to date
   5. Projections and forecasts
   6. Budgets versus actual performance
   7. Inventory analysis
   8. Fixed asset analysis
   9. Cash flow analysis
   10. Debt structure

C. Marketing
   1. Current marketing plan and budgets
   2. Current advertising plan with copies of ads
   3. Customer analysis
   4. Product sales analysis

     5. Geographical sales analysis
       a. Domestic
       b. Export
     6. Sales personnel
       a. Independent representatives (agents)
       b. Sales persons (employees)
     7. Distribution facilities and locations
     8. Market segments
     9. Competition
    10. Copies of all current catalogues, instruction books, parts lists, and other sales or instructional literature
    11. Trade associations

D. Manufacturing
    1. Current manufacturing plan and budgets
    2. Personnel
      a. List of foremen
      b. Engineering
    3. Facilities
      a. Plant, machinery, and equipment
      b. Parking and recreational facilities
      c. Sewage and waste disposal
      d. Utilities
      e. Transportation facilities
    4. Repairs and maintenance
      a. Machine shop
      b. Outside contractors

E. Administration
    1. Administrative personnel
    2. Insurance
      a. Casualty
      b. Liability—public
      c. Liability—product
      d. Employee life, accident, and health
    3. Benefits
      a. Insurance

      b. Pension plan
      c. Vacation policy
      d. Cost analysis of benefits
  4. Personnel
      a. Job titles and job descriptions
      b. Wage and salary policy
      c. Employees' manual and work rules
  5. Accounting
      a. Computer
      b. Personnel
      c. Reports
      d. Fiscal controls
      e. Cash management

The outline of an actual plan made by the seller of a communication company is shown in Appendix C. This company was in a loss situation but projected profitable sales of $5 million within five years. Note how this plan differs from the outline just discussed.

ANALYSIS OF THE TARGET COMPANY

In the second part of the plan the buyer discusses the previously described strengths and weaknesses of the target company and states the course of action he or she would follow after acquiring the company. The buyer must, of course, develop several pro forma financial statements to indicate what he or she thinks the company could do under new leadership in various circumstances. Generally, three detailed pro forma statements for future operations are presented: one under favorable conditions, one for probable conditions, and one for unfavorable conditions. Lenders are influenced by the logic and soundness of these projections:

They must be convinced of the buyer's ability to pay back the loan.

Table 4.1 is an analysis of the profit and loss statement of an acquisition done by a buyer as part of a business plan. The seller had no plan and all financial statements were unaudited and based on "management statements." The figures in column three are pro forma estimates of the buyer. Column four contains comments of the buyer for his own use.

Because these figures were unaudited, the buyer had to satisfy himself that they were reasonable. This was done with the cooperation of the seller and it was determined that the figures were reasonably accurate.

Balance sheet values (book values) of this company were evaluated by the buyer based on estimated fair market value of the assets to be acquired and then values were assigned to these assets to yield a 20% and a 10% return (see Table 4.2).

To do the calculation in column C, assume that you want to yield a 20% pretax return on your investment. To determine what the value of the assets should be, first estimate what the earnings of the company would be under your ownership; Table 4.1 shows this estimate. Let's assume that, after carefully studying several years' profit and loss statements, you decide that you can operate the business to produce a $17,000 profit (before taxes and interest charge for borrowed money are deducted).

Now write down in column C the value of your assets so that they equal five times the pretax return on your investment ($17,000), or $85,000. (Five times estimated pretax earnings is a reasonable multiple to pay for a small manufacturing company.) If you must place values on the assets that are much more than their fair market value (the second column), you may have to assign some of the excess value

TABLE 4.1
Profit and Loss Statement for a Company with Sales of $256,321

Categories	Year Ending 31 December 1986	Pro Forma $250,000	Buyer's Comments
Sales	$256,321	$250,000	Allow for drop in sales
Direct Cost of goods	134,678	140,000	Allow for some slippage in efficiency during the first year
Gross profits	$121,643	$110,000	
Factory Expense			
Indirect labor	$ 15,307	$ 16,000	Allow for raise for foreman (he's important)
Miscellaneous factory expense	5,653	5,000	This can easily be cut down
Depreciation	2,046	2,500	Allow more depreciation because you write up assets
Total factory overhead	$ 23,006	$ 23,500	
General and Administrative Expense			
Officer's salary	$ 20,000	$ 20,000	You can take more (this depends on tax situation)
Office salaries	24,651	12,000	Seller's wife is not necessary on payroll
Telephone	5,385	5,500	Allow for increase, but the figure should be lower
Rent	3,600	3,600	New location is $3,600 a year
Postage	4,187	4,100	You can easily do with less

TABLE 4.1 (continued)

Categories	Year Ending 31 December 1986	Pro Forma $250,000	Buyer's Comments
Professional services	1,650	1,800	You might do with less
Insurance	1,275	1,500	It's better to be safe
Office supplies	2,114	2,000	You can do with less
Payroll tax	2,276	1,800	Wife is not on payroll
Other taxes	1,208	1,500	Allow extra—taxes always go up
Contributions	280	0	Make no gifts
Depreciation	1,096	1,500	Allow more depreciation because you write up assets
Total G and A expenses	$ 67,722	$ 55,300	
Selling expense commissions	$ 1,785	$ 1,700	This remains about the same
Advertising	4,649	6,000	You have some ideas, so it will cost more
Travel and entertainment	10,872	2,500	This is not necessary, but it can help the tax situation
Printing	3,691	4,000	Allow a little more
Total selling expenses	$ 20,997	$ 14,200	
Net income	$ 9,918	$ 17,000	This is too much. Raise your salary or expenses
Interest income	240	0	Seller keeps this small asset
Interest expense	250	7,000	Borrow most of the purchase price
Net income before tax	9,908	10,000	
Federal income tax	1,982	2,000	
Net income after tax	$ 7,926	$ 8,000	

TABLE 4.2
Evaluation Methods

Assets	A Current Book Value	B Fair Market Value	C 20% Return	D 10% Return	E Buyer's Offering Price
Cash	$ 1,537	a	a	a	
Accounts receivable	8,376	a	a	a	
Inventory	57,101	$67,795	$67,795	$ 67,795	
Securities	4,000	a	a	a	
Machinery, equipment	40,420	25,000	15,705	50,000	

Less
  accumulated
  depreciation
	10,395				

Automobile	4,268	1,500	1,500	1,500	

Less
  accumulated
  depreciation
	2,721				

Goodwill[b]					
Total assets	$102,586				

Less cash,
  securities,
  and accounts
  receivable
	13,913				

Total	$ 88,673	$94,295	$85,000	$170,000	

[a]The seller keeps these assets.

[b]Know-how, patents, trade secrets, and trademarks are also considered assets, but no value is assigned to them for these calculations. It's better to pay more for machinery and less for goodwill.

to goodwill (not depreciable). The figures in Table 4.2 are, of course, arbitrary.

Assuming that profits remain the same, you may be satisfied with a pretax return on your investment of 10%. If this is so, go to column D and value the assets so that they total $170,000. In this case, the values do not seem justified because the goodwill is not deductible and because 10% is really a small return on your investment.

If you have correctly figured the true earning power of the

company to be somewhere between $10,000 and $20,000 per year before taxes (as the actual profit and loss statement and your pro forma in Table 4.1 show), a fair price for the business would range from $50,000 to $100,000. If you feel confident that you can easily increase sales and earnings, $85,000 would be a bargain price for the business (if you think in terms of future benefits, which should rightly accrue only to the buyer and not to the seller).

Study these figures; note how the total value of the assets varies according to the point of view taken. Try to put yourself in the position of the seller. What values do you think he or she might assign to the assets? How would the seller react to the values you have assigned to them?

Now make one more column (E) of values: the price that you are willing to pay for the assets. When you arrive at this total, decide how much less the seller might accept. Then go ahead and make your initial offer.

Because of the total lack of preparation on the part of the seller and the risk involved in accepting unaudited figures, the buyer made an initial offer of $30,000 for this business. The seller thought that she ought to get $50,000; however, she was anxious to sell the business. The buyer raised his offer to $35,000 and the seller quickly lowered her price to $40,000. They were both obviously in the same ballpark and the result was a final price of $37,750 with the seller taking $17,750 at closing and a note for $20,000 due one year after closing.

The seller was in a weak position in this deal and her lack of preparation probably cost her $20,000. It is interesting to note that, although the buyer was never able to increase sales significantly, he was able to reduce costs substantially (which he was counting on) so that the earnings of this company were nearly twice the projected figure. The company was again sold 10 years later for $180,000.

The principal concern of the lender is cash flow. In addi-

TABLE 4.3
Cash Flow Analysis[a]

Average Estimated Monthly Expenses	
Direct cost (labor and materials)	$11,666
Indirect labor	1,333
Miscellaneous factor expense	417
Officer's salary	1,667
Office salaries	1,000
Telephone	458
Rent	300
Postage	341
Office supplies	167
Payroll tax	150
Other taxes	125
Commissions	142
Advertising	500
Travel and entertainment	208
Printing	333
Interest expense	583
Total	$19,390

[a]The one-time expenses for insurance, income tax, and professional services ($1,500, $2,000, and $1,800 respectively) are not included in average monthly expenses.

tion to a comprehensive description and analysis of the target company the lender wants to see how he can get regular and dependable payments on his loan.

Table 4.3 shows the monthly cash flow estimate of the company analyzed in Tables 4.1 and 4.2. Based on this projection the buyer should budget a $25,000 per month cash flow requirement in his planning.

Dealing with Lawyers, Accountants, Bankers, and Partners

When the plan and pro forma statements are complete and done well, you should be able to see very clearly how much capital is needed for equity and debt. If you have the equity contribution and a convincing plan with ample cash flow from the target company, the lender will advance you some money. How much will depend on how good a salesperson you are. If it's a good-looking deal in all respects, you will probably not have to give up any equity to a bank. You will have to give up some equity if you're talking to partners, private investors, or venture capital groups. If you don't like any of the lender's proposals (they usually ask for a pretty big piece of the action), talk to some of your talented friends. They might be a lot less demanding. Whether you're a buyer or seller, even if you can bring the deal to a definitive agreement by yourself, you should not try to close the deal without a lawyer, accountant, and financial advisor (generally a banker).

For the seller a good tight legal agreement is advisable, with the tax consequences well known in advance and your financial future carefully planned.

The buyer must avoid hidden liabilities or unanticipated obligations, unfavorable tax consequences, and unexpected disappointments due to poor advice, poor planning, or inexcusable oversights.

In addition to the absolute necessity of lawyers and accountants and the prudence of investment experts, you may want to consider teaming up with someone who has talents in areas where your abilities are only pedestrian. This is especially appropriate in a larger business (annual sales over $1 million) where there is outside financing.

In some cases, a partner might be only an investor, but banks like enterprises where all partners are talented, compatible, complementary, and active in the business. This gives them a high "comfort factor" that may be critical in their investment decision.

In order to be successful, multiple principals who are employees in a manufacturing business must all be effective managers. A small company cannot afford to have a single manager who is ineffective. It is important, therefore, to have partners with superior management qualifications as well as capital.

Gathering Information

A good plan requires lots of information and it's better to have too much than too little. It's also better to have the data well organized and easy to understand (charts and graphs are usually recognized as a sign of a careful and thorough organizer).

As a buyer, you must do the bulk of the work and ask all the right questions. Actually the buyer and the seller are in a sense partners during a large part of the negotiations because they both must work together to convince a lender to finance the deal.

The information provided by the seller is only the beginning of what is needed to close a successful deal. The buyer needs information on the industry in which the target company operates. There are numerous sources of information, of which the following are only a few:

SIC (Standard Industrial Classification)

Many years ago the U.S. Government developed the Standard Industrial Classification Manual to promote the comparability of statistics describing various facets of the economy of the nation. Developed initially for use within government for statistical purposes, the SIC is now widely used by business firms for classification of their customers and suppliers in market research. The SIC Manual is sold by the Superintendent of Documents, U.S. Government Printing Office, Washington, D.C. 20402.

If you want to research any industry or segment of an industry, you can find an SIC number to identify that industry and that number can then be used to locate companies in the industry. For example, dish cloths made in knitting mills have the SIC number 2259, dish cloths made in weaving mills have 2211, and nonwoven dish cloths have 2392.

If you want to know how many companies are included under each SIC number, send for the catalog of the mailing list compilers (SIC 7331), who classify their lists by SIC numbers. If you want to know the names and addresses of these companies, you order the mailing list ($20–$50 per thousand names). You will often find quantities and names listed by state.

Directories

B. Klein & Company, 104 Fifth Avenue, New York, New York 10011 publishes a *Guide to American Directories*. This is an indispensable reference book (found in most libraries) showing you where to go to get lists of companies, institutions, people, and so on. If you are interested in acquisition or buyer prospects only in Connecticut, for example, you can get:

Connecticut Products and Services. Containing about 1000 Connecticut manufacturers and distributors of products and services.

Connecticut South Central Region: An Economic Profile and Industrial Directory. A list of 1066 New Haven area manufacturers.

Directory of Connecticut Manufacturing and Mechanical Establishments. 6000 Connecticut manufacturers and registered mechanical firms.

State of Connecticut Classified Business Directory. 43,000 Connecticut manufacturers, wholesalers, distributors, banks, institutions, schools and colleges, retailers, brokers, insurance companies, restaurants, and so on.

If you want to do some research on a particular product or industry, you can often find a directory that relates directly to your interest. For example, a few of the many directories that are available include:

Oil well drilling contractors
Lumber dealers in Indiana
Forging plants
Hydroelectric power plants
Libraries in Oklahoma
Mail order businesses
Metalworking machinery manufacturers
Foundries in the United States
Potato growers
Trade associations
Glove manufacturers

These directories are not only a valuable research source for the buyer or seller of companies, but are also indispensable for the marketing manager of a small manufacturing company. From a list of directories, the marketing manager can select dozens (perhaps hundreds) that will list his or her products or services often at no charge. The author's company and its products are presently listed in over 200 directories and buyers' guides. These listings are coded so we can tell the source of inquiries or orders. They produce sales.

Thomas Register

This directory is listed in the *Guide to American Directories* and contains a list of over 100,000 manufacturers along with an estimate of their capital assets. There is also a classified listing of over 1 million products. The directory is revised annually and old copies can be picked up from friends or associates who subscribe to the service. Many libraries have copies.

Chambers of Commerce

Johnson Publishing Company, Box 455, Loveland, Colorado 80537 publishes a list of about 5000 chambers of commerce in the United States. This is a valuable source of commercial and industrial information on specific localities in which you might be interested. Most chambers of commerce publish a list of manufacturing and commercial companies in their community with details on the size, number of employees, and products or services. We find these lists to be a valuable source of acquisition prospects.

There should be an estimate of the market share of the target company, the size and location of the market, and the future prospects for the market (shrinking, expanding, or static). You also should analyze the competition, research information on the significant competitors, and discuss the state of the art. To get this knowledge you can visit competitors, get their sales literature, talk to people in the trade associations, and do some research in technical libraries. Frequently you will find business school professors who specialize in a particular industry. These people are not only good sources of information but may be able to lead you to prospective partners, investors, or other advisors.

Also you may occasionally find a business broker who is very knowledgeable in certain areas or industries. He or she is anxious to use that knowledge and can provide valuable information not only on specific companies but in the fine art of buying or selling.

Education

One of the greatest dangers in buying a small manufacturing company is the lack of knowledge of the target company and of the industry of which it is a part.

A seller probably spent most of his or her working career in this industry and knows it intimately. The seller will tell you about all the good things and very little of the bad. You must educate yourself quickly and determine how much of the seller's success or failure is due to his or her own personal ability or lack of ability and how much is due to factors completely beyond his or her control.

If you recognize weaknesses in the seller's management that resulted in missed opportunities and if you know that you can do better, the chances are that you can be successful even if the industry has negative factors (all industries have some). But when you see a highly talented manager who has done everything right and has not been successful, the uncontrollable negative factors may be overwhelming. Most talented managers are smart enough to avoid such situations; but if they do get involved in a bad deal, the only way they can redeem themselves is to sell the mess to an unsophisticated buyer for a fancy price.

A very interesting new entrepreneurial idea has recently developed among larger companies in the United States: starting captive entrepreneurial businesses. In other words, your partner could be your employer!

Small companies have always had the advantage of being free of bureaucracy and most of the other fetters of big business and complex organizations. IBM and Westing-house among others are now encouraging and financing small satellite businesses within their organization but free of the usual parental constraints. Of course, there is an element of self-interest in this idea. Theoretically the entrepreneur is supposed to develop benefits for the corporate sponsor.

5

Planning
for the Seller

Chapter 2 discussed the valuation of the seller's company and some ways to look for a buyer. It was assumed there that the company could offer attractive advantages to a prospective buyer. After a careful and honest analysis, the seller may decide that it would be better to liquidate his or her company assets, pay off creditors, and retire. But there may be other alternatives.

Among the many factors in a business opportunity, successful buyers look for good earnings (or an obvious potential for good earnings), valuable assets, competent employees, favorable location, and growth potential. Are any of these factors missing in your business? Could they be added or corrected? Can you modify your operations to improve the buyer's perception?

GOOD EARNINGS

A knowledgeable buyer of a small manufacturing business expects to make a profit, either in operating the business, merging it into another business owned by the buyer, or selling it to someone else. The buyer therefore wants to know how profitable the business has been for the seller. The profit and loss statement provides this information.

If poor profits are shown, the buyer will make an offer based on the low profit unless the seller can clearly show that profits are "hidden" or taken out of the business in large salaries or unjustified expenses. To avoid having to explain why a profitable business doesn't show decent profits, a seller should consider allowing hidden profits to show (not excessively) on the profit and loss statement. The seller does not necessarily have to sell cash or cash equivalents to a buyer unless the common stock is sold and then the cash can be recovered in a higher price.

If the company really has marginal profits then the seller ought to consider making an effort to improve profitability for a few years prior to sale. This requires planning and perhaps some sacrifice, but if successful the seller can get a better price for the company.

VALUABLE ASSETS

Valuable assets are such things as modern, energy-efficient buildings in attractive locations; well-maintained state-of-the-art machinery and equipment; a balanced inventory which turns over three or four times per year with low obsolescence; loyal and steady customers; dependable suppliers; a reputation for high quality, good service, and prompt deliveries; and so on.

These assets have obvious earning power in a successful

manufacturing company and it is not difficult for the buyer to perceive this value.

COMPETENT EMPLOYEES

Many successful manufacturers attribute their success not to their production or their modern facilities but to their employees: the employees who work in the factory, design and engineer the products, talk to customers and prospects, control the quality, pack and ship carefully, and do all the things necessary to produce and sell a desirable product at a reasonable price.

Competent employees are chosen carefully by competent management. They are trained by skilled leaders and compensated fairly. The character of the enterprise can be judged by its employees.

FAVORABLE LOCATION

Some companies are for sale because the work place is so miserable that the company cannot attract decent workers or managers. It may also suffer from a high factory overhead because of crowding, disorder, dangerous conditions, low-energy efficiency, and so forth.

Other unfavorable locations are those in very high cost areas, congested areas with poor parking and public transportation facilities.

Favorable locations include areas where reasonable housing is available for employees, as well as good schools and other community services. Local taxes are another location factor that must be considered.

In most cases where location is an important factor, moving the operation may be the only solution. Although there

are risks in moving a manufacturing operation, it is frequently done. We have moved five companies (or product
lines) without serious difficulty and in every case the move
had noticeable, positive effects on the operation.

GROWTH POTENTIAL

Most sellers of small manufacturing companies will spend
a lot of time in trying to convince a prospective buyer that
the business offered for sale has tremendous potential. The
seller will also have a good story to tell the buyer to explain
why the potential has not been achieved.

Judging the growth potential is entirely the responsibility
of the buyer. This judgment is based solely on the buyer's
knowledge and experience and is probably the greatest single risk factor in buying a small manufacturing business.

INFORMATION

Every knowledgeable buyer of a small manufacturing company has a checklist of desired information about the target
company. This list is different for every prospect but usually
includes the following five categories.

Five or More Years of Detailed Certified
Audited Financial Statements

If these are not prepared by a certified public accountant the
buyer will probably ask to have a personal accountant look

at the books and perhaps do a certified audit and inventory test. Without certified audits, the buyer will have less confidence in the unaudited figures. Audits with serious qualifications, such as "inventory per estimate of management," are almost as bad as none. When planning to sell your business, start having certified audits by independent auditors several years beforehand.

A Detailed List of All Important Assets

The balance sheet assets of items of machinery, equipment, and vehicles should be detailed separately so that the buyer can look at every item. The list should show the age of the item, purchase date, and make and book value.

A List of All Suppliers

An alphabetical list of all your suppliers should be provided together with total annual purchases from each one. For high-volume suppliers, you should list the principal items purchased (such as machined parts, catalogs, custodial services, packing and shipping materials). If any equipment of yours, such as tooling, dies, or moulds, is held by your suppliers, be sure to list it.

A Look at Accounts Receivable

Inasmuch as receivables change daily, a complete list is not necessary but the buyer should be allowed to look through the receivable ledger accounts (cards or computer printouts). He or she should also be provided with a list by customers and amount of all overdue accounts. This is standard practice in most businesses and if the information is not available, the seller should certainly set up a system to supply a monthly report on overdue accounts for management. Any prospective buyer is going to want this information.

Marketing Information

There are many marketing records that prospective buyers want to see. If you don't have them, an astute buyer will ask you to make some estimates and probably offer less for the business. Among the important sales records frequently asked for are the following:

1. A list of all directly served customers showing several years' annual sales to each of these customers.
2. A list of all dealers, agents, and representatives. These should be available with records and commentary on performance. Names, addresses, telephone numbers, and personal information should be available on all key personnel in the dealer, agent, or representative organization. If there are important market areas in which you have low or no sales, you should have lists of prospective dealers and your marketing plan (see below) should show how you expect to improve sales in these areas.
3. A list of major product lines (by model number, style, size, or color) showing annual sales of each line.
4. A list of all important market segments by industry (where known) such as aerospace, transportation, foundries, hospitals, schools, woodworking, and metalworking.

5. A list of all export accounts by country.

6. A geographical breakdown of domestic sales (where appropriate) by state.

Other marketing records for buyers whose background is marketing should be made available, such as:

7. Copies of past and current advertisements, direct-mail pieces, and other promotional material (including packaging and labeling).

8. Copies of current catalogs, price lists, bulletins, news releases, product data, and application data sheets.

9. Instruction books, parts lists, and owners manuals.

10. Warranties, logotypes, and letterheads.

11. Product photographs, artwork, printing mechanicals, and so on.

12. Marketing plans and budgets with advertising schedules. One of the most common causes of failure in small manufacturing companies is insufficient orders. Any knowledgeable buyer is going to want to know how to expand the business and how you achieved marketing success. A good marketing plan will provide this information. This plan should cover 12 months. It should have reasonable sales goals with an affordable budget (expressed as a percentage of sales) to implement the plan. It should spell out where sales volume can be increased and how it's going to be done. There should also be a record of past sales achievements compared to forecasts to prove that a carefully planned marketing program can produce results. Nothing can instill more confidence in a business than records of steady, dependable growth in sales and earnings.

Manufacturing Records

These records should include engineering drawings, specifications, bills of material, flow sheets, inventory records, manufacturing process or operation data, work standards, and so on.

Cost Records

If asked what the cost of a product is, can you show a standard procedure that accurately determines costs? A buyer will also want to know how indirect (overhead) costs are figured and applied. These should be easily available and up-to-date for all products.

Copyrights, Patents, Contracts, and Agreements

All important corporate documents should be kept in a safe place and be available in original or copy form to any buyer who wishes to see them. These should include contracts within the corporation (e.g., employment) or between the corporation and outside entities such as large sales contracts, union contracts, stockholder agreements, and joint venture agreements.

Historical records are also of interest to some buyers and these can sometimes be of significant value in selling a business.

A List of All Key Employees

Many key employees continue in the employ of a new owner when a business is sold. Therefore it is important for a prospective buyer to know who these key people are, what their pay and perks are, and what their responsibilities and duties are. The best way to present this information is with a detailed job description (see Appendix B) and a performance evaluation record. It is also important to supply a job description of the chief executive, regardless of whether he or she stays.

Fringe Benefits

Even small companies today have enough fringe benefits to justify an employees' manual. Such a manual, among other things, specifies exactly the benefits to which employees are entitled. Common ones include health and life insurance, paid holidays, vacation time, and savings or stock purchase plans.

Company Policy Manual

Few small companies have a company policy manual, yet it can be a very useful management tool and a helpful document when you sell your company. This manual is a written guide for the organization and operation of the manufacturing enterprise. It contains not only management philosophy but company work rules, policies, procedures, and guidelines from administration, manufacturing, and marketing practices and standards to philanthropy and social responsibilities.

A good company policy manual that has been actively followed can answer more questions from a prospective buyer of your company than any other single document.

DEFICIENCY CORRECTION

Few small companies have all of the records and materials that are described above. Furthermore, some prospective buyers of your business would have no interest in a number of the areas of information listed. But most owners of small manufacturing companies would agree that these types of information could be useful if not valuable. They would also argue, however, that it is difficult to have all this information up-to-date and readily available at a moment's notice.

It has been our experience in interviews and visits with hundreds of small-company owners that the majority are ill-prepared to sell their companies and that they cannot furnish even 25% of the sorts of information that a buyer would like to have in an orderly fashion.

Some sellers of small manufacturing businesses are aware of the constantly growing demand for companies like theirs and they do not feel that it is worthwhile to furnish any other information than financial statements together with a willingness to answer any questions that a prospective buyer may have. This attitude leads to a lot of negative answers when the buyer asks for sales records, job descriptions, and manufacturing procedures that the seller cannot furnish. In some cases the buyer will either walk away from the opportunity or lower his or her perceived value of the enterprise.

The negative impact of a limited information flow can be softened if the seller creates a few of the more important elements of information. For example, a good marketing plan might impress a prospect enough to offset the lack of good engineering drawings or job descriptions. Other areas where the seller can make improvements in the business to present a more salable image include the following:

Housekeeping

Real estate agents tell home sellers to "spruce up" the house and grounds before showing it to prospects. This advice applies to manufacturing companies even more than to dwelling houses. Reliable buyers take notice of disorderly and unattractive offices and factories. They look for safety violations, environmental problems, work place hazards, and employee discontent. Try to eliminate unfavorable visual aspects of your company before offering it for sale.

Record Keeping

All records requested by the buyer should be up-to-date and readily available in businesslike form. Some buyers, especially owners of other companies, are not only seeking to expand their sales by acquisition but they may expect to acquire experienced and skilled management. If you want an on-going relationship with the new owner (as a director, consultant, or employee) you must sell the idea that you will be a valuable or indispensable asset. Even if you are not invited to stay with the new owner, you should prepare a proforma profit and loss statement for the next 12 months based on reasonable expectations that could be achieved by competent management.

Long-Range Preparations

The wise owner will plan for the sale of the business several years before seeking buyers. He or she should also anticipate taking as much as one or two years to find a suitable buyer. Most small manufacturing company owners do not allow anywhere near that much time and they generally fail to receive a fair price. Selling your business requires meticulous and often laborious planning.

If your profit and loss statements do not show attractive earnings, you should try to reduce expenses and/or improve sales. If your product quality has deteriorated, you should try to improve it. If your managers and workers are indifferent and insufficiently productive, you should provide training and motivational programs. If you can't reach these goals yourself, hire someone to do it for you.

Is your company carefully controlled with competent middle management and good planning, or does it tend to be crisis-oriented with daily emergencies and unanticipated problems? If you have constant interruptions, frantic telephone calls, endless and fruitless meetings, and have to work nights and weekends, try to delegate responsibility to control this turmoil. The character of your company is revealed to a prospective buyer through visits to the work place. You should present a picture of orderliness, efficiency, and control by good management. Anything less reduces the value of your business.

THE BUYER'S PERCEPTION

Your valuation of your own business will probably be higher than that of a prospective buyer. If not, someone has done something wrong or there are mental reservations by one or both parties. The price and terms at which the deal is finally executed are a matter of negotiation in which one party probably has an advantage over the other. Will you be the one with the advantage? That depends on the perceptions of the buyer. If the buyer thinks that your company is the best one to buy, you probably have the advantage.

6

How to Find Opportunities

In 1975 I estimated (using Dun & Bradstreet figures) that there were about 185,000 small manufacturing companies in the United States with annual sales of $100,000 to $500,000. I used this sales range at that time because companies of that size could be interesting to manage and could support an owner/manager comfortably.

In 1986 I expanded my estimates (with the help of Dun & Bradstreet) to 90,000 small manufacturing companies in the United States with sales of $500,000 to $1 million. Sales of less than $500,000 are very small companies these days. At any given time at least 10% (or about 9000) of these companies are for sale. For Canada my business uses a ratio of 10:1, which means there might be 9000 such companies in Canada with about 900 for sale.

Purchase of manufacturing companies in foreign countries

by U.S. citizens adds a very high degree of risk above the ordinary business risk. There is no scarcity of opportunities in the United States, however, and you will find them in every state.

DESCRIBING YOUR REQUIREMENTS

Most business brokers like to have a general description of the type of business you are seeking. We have found that too specific a description reduces the number and quality of opportunities but insufficient detail can waste time. Here are some suggestions on parameters and priorities you must establish (these should be identified in order of importance):

Size of company	$500,000–$750,000 annual sales; not over 50 employees; must need no more than 10,000 square feet
Principal product (specific or general)	Saw blades; reciprocating saw blades; circular saw blades; saw blades, handles, and frames; hand saws; table saws; band saws; woodworking tools; woodworking machinery; woodworking equipment; portable power tools, woodworking
Location	Within 50 miles of Memphis, Tennessee; Tulsa, Oklahoma; New England; Sun Belt; west of Mississippi; not important
Profitability	10% on sales before state and federal taxes; potential of 10% pretax on sales; not important
Real estate	Must have owned or leased building and land; must have room for expan-

	sion; none required (buyer will move operations)
Management	Management (except seller) to stay; seller to stay for one year
Purchase	Only certain assets; 100% of stock; 51% of stock

NETWORKING

With the advent of personal computers and data banks in the late 1970s and early 1980s, an old activity has been recognized and termed *networking*. This can be roughly defined as the gathering, sorting, and dissemination of information, often with the aid of computers but more frequently by personal contact, telephone, or mail.

Some networks are "closed." These deal with private, confidential information that is compiled for very special and sometimes illegal purposes. However, most networks are open and easily accessible to anyone who wants to join.

In searching for a business acquisition opportunity, you must have as many sources of information as possible. The best way to secure this information is to set up your own network. Start with your lawyer, banker, and accountant. They will surely know of businesses for sale (sometimes because the businesses are in trouble). They will help you because they have a vested interest in your welfare: The more prosperous you are the better you are as a client.

To these primary sources of reliable information add secondary sources of somewhat less reliable but voluminous information, such as:

Friends and relatives

Business acquaintances

Business consultants

Insurance agents

Business and trade association executives

Chambers of commerce

State and local industrial development agencies

SBICs

Other private investors

Finally, you must contact business brokers, answer ads of businesses for sale (*The Wall Street Journal, The New York Times,* etc.), place ads in suitable publications (trade papers, local newspapers, etc.) and make direct personal contact with companies that you might like to own.

A serious buyer should have at least 50 sources of information in his or her network. Offering a modest finder's fee to a special source often brings more good prospects. For a seller of a business, the search for potential buyers is treated in Chapter 2.

IDENTIFYING PROSPECTS

Any good salesperson makes cold calls on worthwhile prospects. If you want to acquire or sell a business, you're going to have to get out into the marketplace and make a deal. There are several ways in which you can locate and qualify businesses that might be for sale:

1. You can go to a prospect's place of business (A) and ask him or her to let you have a few minutes to discuss an idea. Tell the prospect that you want to buy a manufacturing company (B) that serves his or her industry. This could

be one of the prospect's suppliers. If you can gain his or her confidence, the prospect may reveal which suppliers are the most unsatisfactory. If there are any that interest you, you have a prospect and you know one of the prospect's customers. Now this doesn't mean that the prospect is qualified—qualified prospects must be willing to consider selling their company or, at least, talk with you about it.

In addition to getting this information, you may have planted an idea in the mind of the owner of business (A): "Should I think about selling my business?" or, "I might be able to find out what my business is worth." Many owners of small manufacturing businesses are woefully ignorant of the fine art of estimating fair market values on their assets. If they have thought at all about the ultimate fate of their business, they have made an attempt to put a value on it. They have also realized that valuing intangible assets is a difficult thing to do. You can provide them with valuable knowledge by helping to educate them.

2. After careful study of the target company (A), you can develop a plan for your acquisition of the supplier (B). Go over this plan with the owner of (A) and suggest (at an appropriate time) that you might be willing to merge your acquisition (B) into company (A), with the idea that you would eventually buy owner (A) out and control (A) and (B).

3. In productive networks acquisition prospect leads are exchanged between buyers. We have current files on nearly 300 target companies, and any buyer that I have ever met has shown remarkable interest in these data. Invariably the buyer offers to let me see his or her files if we will reciprocate. We have acquired two companies in this way.

The best way to construct files is to file acquisition prospects alphabetically and on two sets of index cards: one organized by product and industry, the other by size (annual sales) and price (or estimated value). This, of course, can be done on your home computer and put "on line" if you are networking with other computer owners who have transmitting and receiving modems. Our files are far more extensive than those of many business brokers but they must be carefully controlled and kept confidential. We do not allow anyone to look at our files without first checking with the target company. Several sales to third parties have been consummated as a result of our system, and in all cases buyers and sellers seem well matched and pleased.

Some people who want to buy a manufacturing company think good prospects ought to be easy to find. They're not. For every good acquisition prospect, there are dozens of sophisticated buyers. Since 1958 we have bought nine companies or product lines. To satisfy our fairly demanding requirements, we looked at approximately 900 prospects. Many of these "looks" took five minutes or less to determine that we weren't interested.

If you want a steady flow of prospects, you will see a lot of turkeys but you must not get impatient with your sources of information. Good prospects show up at odd times and unlikely places. If you tell a broker (or other networker) that you're interested in manufacturing companies that make wood products, you may get a call with a sweet deal on a grey iron foundry. Don't turn the broker off. Thank him or her and put the foundry in your file for trading.

Each suggested source of information discussed previously can produce valuable leads if properly handled, but each one requires some sort of incentive if you want to get their best efforts. As we indicated, a finder's fee might help, mutual interests with other investors are valuable, and the prospect of a new business in town is what industrial development agencies want.

One of the most valuable members of our acquisition network is an insurance agent who specializes in estate planning for owners of small manufacturing companies. Life insurance provides a way to reduce estate taxes and many successful small-business owners find themselves facing this problem as they consider the future of their business and the welfare of their heirs. A life insurance audit with an older business owner often triggers thoughts about selling the business. We have an arrangement with several insurance agents to exchange prospects for our mutual benefit and have had enough success to consider this a useful way to find prospects for insurance and acquisitions.

SEARCHING FOR PRODUCTS

If you have any special interest in a particular industry or product, you should do some serious research among the reference books, directories, and trade papers that serve that industry or product. Look at the advertising, read the classified section of Thomas Register, and check product lists published by chambers of commerce in any place in which you would like to locate your manufacturing business.

If location is your prime objective, then you would of course have to find out what companies are in the area you have chosen. However, some small manufacturing companies are easy to move and many that are for sale are in fact moved from inner city and blighted areas to rural locations. We have moved three companies from highly congested downtown locations in large cities to a small New England town. We moved one south from its original location on the Canadian border.

Large manufacturing companies buy from thousands of small companies. Contacts in these large companies will often reveal what products or services they need and whether or not there might be an opportunity to start your manufacturing career by being an independent supplier to a larger company.

Most entrepreneurs do not consider product to be an important factor. They search for opportunities—which they often find in product lines and locations that they don't expect.

7

Distress Situations

The high risk of entrepreneurial business is reflected in bankruptcy reports, many of which involve small manufacturing companies. In the anxious months preceding a bankruptcy, the unfortunate business owners and their creditors are frantically trying to rescue the enterprise. The value is shrinking rapidly, emergency action is being taken, the lenders have retreated into their "work-out" position—doom and gloom is everywhere.

Any outsider who appears on the scene of extreme unction with a rescue plan is apt to be labeled a vulture. If you don't mind being called a vulture, there are some interesting opportunities for the entrepreneur, especially Mr. Fixit who likes handyman specials.

Creditors like to talk to rescuers who have some reasonable ideas about how to salvage a foundering company.

Banks are especially pleased to find someone interested, especially a well-managed, financially sound company that has the resources and experience to effect a turnaround. And the banks will generally pay a handsome price to find a solution to their problem.

The hopeless owners will also agree to relinquish control if there is a reasonable assurance of avoiding bankruptcy and salvaging a few crumbs of equity.

These situations are not for the fainthearted or those who have achieved and wish to maintain a high comfort factor. They are dangerous situations but they can often be handled with 50-cent dollars for high-tax-bracket companies or individuals. In addition to sheltering taxable dollars, there may be real bargains for capital assets such as machinery, patents, buildings, and land. Another advantage could be a moratorium on payments to creditors or settlements of less than the full amount on trade liabilities, especially if the creditors have lost all hope and have written off the receivable as uncollectible.

For the handy person who works well under pressure and has confidence in his or her own ability to resolve complex problems in a highly emotional atmosphere, the rewards can be extremely high (so are the risks).

The most logical starting point to help save a distressed company is with the prime lender, usually a bank. You simply present your credentials to one of the loan officers and ask how many clients need experienced management help. In some cases the bank is in virtual control of the troubled company and can put you in as a consultant (fee contingent on results) or as a member of the board of directors or even as an officer. These latter two options expose you to especially serious risk because there may be personal or official financial liability and possibly criminal liability if the company has violated any laws.

The next best contacts to make when you are looking for distress situations are lawyers and accountants. Every company in trouble has to turn to their legal and financial advisors at a fairly early stage (generally before a full-blown crisis). This is the best time to start work on a rescue plan. This "critical decision point" could easily be the last chance that management has to save the operation and its self-respect.

Lawyers and accountants do not reveal confidential client information to strangers; therefore, you will have to cultivate some informal relationships with these professionals whereby you can be introduced or recommended to the target companies.

Dissension among owners often causes poor performance in small companies even though nothing is basically wrong with the company or the product. This is not a direct cause of bankruptcy although it could lead to it. The company might appear to be in trouble with diminishing sales, expenses out of control, and inadequate cash flow. The only solution to this problem could be a new owner or a third-party advisor who could see solutions that the feuding owners don't perceive. This situation would probably not be regarded as a serious crisis by creditors, lawyers, or accountants; nevertheless, it would be an acquisition opportunity for the discerning entrepreneur. The best way to find out about such opportunities is from one of the owners—which means you've got to get to know business owners.

You can avoid the vulture label by being the intermediary in a negotiation between a strong buyer and a weakened seller, then taking your reward in common stock of the buyer. This tactic sometimes takes the onus off the buyer, who is assuming a large risk for the vague possibility of future benefit and at the same time helping to reduce otherwise inevitable economic losses.

Correct analysis of the distress situation prior to acquisition is obviously of critical importance. There is no opportunity for a second chance and no room for error. The analysis procedures detailed in Chapter 8 for a normal acquisition opportunity should be modified to assume the worst possible scenario for the failing prospect. Use a falling sales projection, add contingencies for extra legal and accounting expenses, and try to reduce overhead expenses to the absolute minimum.

Successful entrepreneurs quickly learn crisis management and it's always helpful to learn at someone else's expense.

8

Evaluating the Opportunity

PRELIMINARY ANALYSIS

Acquisitions that appear to be attractive at first blush require time for analysis. This can take anywhere from an hour up to several days. If you're intrigued with the prospectus and financials, then you'll have to go look at the company and talk to the owner.

After you've studied 20 or 30 proposals, you begin to develop an analysis procedure that cuts through all the irrelevant, useless, and misleading material you generally receive at the outset. (Note to sellers: Present your company to the prospective buyer in the most favorable way you can without exaggeration or weak excuses for poor performance.)

A preliminary analysis of the target company should be documented as a report to the buyer's advisors or investors.

A typical example is shown in Appendix A. From this experience you can prepare your own checklist on the factors you consider important. You also should make a list of standard questions that you want the owner to answer. Here are some suggestions:

Marketing

1. Is there a marketing plan? Can you see it?
2. Are there copies of all ads and catalogs?
3. Is there a customer list? Can you look at it?
4. Who are the 50 best customers?
5. Are there good sales statistics:
   a. By customer?
   b. By product?
   c. By geographical area?
6. Is there a list of prospects?
7. What markets could the owner sell to that are not now being served?
8. What is the current market share?
9. Is there a list of competitors and their literature?

Manufacturing

1. Are there good drawings and specifications on all products?
2. How about a list of suppliers?
3. Is the inventory all usable and balanced?
4. How fast does the inventory turn over?
5. What about customer service and repairs?

Research and Development

1. Does the owner have ideas for new products or applications?

2. Is the technology at the leading or trailing edge?

3. Is the company an innovative leader or a follower?

Administration

1. Does the owner have a formal written budget for sales, expenses, cash flow?

2. Are there monthly comparisons of actual performance against budget?

3. Are there good key people in administration such as office manager, bookkeeper, and controller?

4. Do orders get entered quickly and correctly?

5. What is the average collection period? Thirty days (excellent), 45 days (good), 60 days (fair), more than 60 days (watch out!).

6. How many employees have cars, expense accounts, or company loans?

This list is only a general guide. There are many more questions that may be appropriate. The buyer must develop his or her own procedures and style in all encounters with prospective sellers. The single most important factor is that the buyer must convey to a seller a strong sense of mutual trustworthiness. If this is not accomplished, a fair deal can rarely be put together.

HAS THE OWNER PREPARED THE BUSINESS FOR SALE?

In our experience, most owners of small manufacturing businesses tend to carry far too much information in their hats and therefore cannot show you plans, budgets, sales forecasts, and meaningful statistics. Unfortunately this is to their distinct disadvantage when it comes time to sell their business because these figures must then be hastily reconstructed from poor records or, worse, cannot be made available. In that case, the seller can make up estimates but the buyer will certainly discount them to some degree.

WHAT IS THE RISK?

The risk of buying a small manufacturing business is expressed by the formula $R = \sqrt{-1}$: indeterminate. An incompetent or dishonest management can destroy a successful company in very short order. A weak management can be carried along for years with a good product, some skilled middle managers, and a few lucky breaks. A few rough guidelines can be provided:

1. If the business has been in existence for many years and had reasonably good earnings, you can assume that it has achieved a certain momentum that can probably be maintained at a fairly low risk by competent management. If a buyer sees obvious ways to improve and expand the business, the risk is even lower.

2. If the company shows no significant earnings and large withdrawals by the owner (salary, perquisites, etc.), it may be a low or moderate risk situation but the buyer must certainly do a pro forma profit and loss projection to see if these expenses could be reallocated to improve the business.

3. If the owner takes home a modest salary and the earnings of the company are poor, the buyer must determine if this is due to bad management, competitive pressure, or some faulty bookkeeping. The situation could be high risk.

4. The buyer should be knowledgeable about risks in comparative investments. Here are a few examples:

Type of Investment	After-Tax Annual Return	Risk Factor
Savings accounts	4 – 5%	Low
Government securities	4 – 10%	Low
Municipal bonds	4 – 10%	Low
Commercial paper	6 – 9%	Low
Mortgages	8 – 13%	Low to moderate
Blue chip common stock	5 – 10%	Moderate
Common stock mutual funds	5 – 10%	Moderate
Growth stocks	10 – 20%	High
Real estate ownership	10 – 50%	High
Raw land ownership	10 – 100%	High
Small manufacturing company (over seven years in business)	10 – 25%	High
Start-up manufacturing company (no record of earnings)	−100 – +100%	Very high
Commodities	−100 – +500%	Extremely high
Gambling	−100 to ?	Extremely high

WHAT IS THE EARNING POWER?

The true earning power of a business enterprise is the profit it can generate under the most competent management—

not, as is often assumed, under ideal conditions. Ideal conditions seldom exist and certainly never exist in exactly the right order and magnitude. Competent management proves its value by operating successfully under all conditions.

In evaluating a small business to determine its earning power under a new management, you have to study its past performance and try to judge the level of competence required to produce the record of performance. Then you ask yourself if you would have done better or worse and how you think you might do if you bought the business.

One important element of success in acquiring and operating a small business is your ability to identify and modify things that the seller is not doing well. The first place to look for information is in the profit and loss statement (see Table 4.1). Every item of expense must be carefully analyzed to find out the following:

1. *How Are Figures Determined?* You must understand how the owner arrived at the figures so that you can find elements of cost that you can eliminate or control. You must remember that an owner/manager is constantly seeking ways to minimize taxes. He or she will charge all expenses legally possible to the enterprise in order to reduce tax liability.

2. *How Do Expenses Compare with Other Similar Businesses?* It is desirable to compare the performance of the target company with other similar business. Comparable figures might come from a business with which you are presently associated or from other businesses to which you might have access. Performance data of closely held businesses are difficult to come by and you may have to develop them yourself. Trade associations and publications, case studies (from business schools), or figures from public companies might be helpful.

If you are lucky enough to find obvious evidence of poor management judgment or errors, you should make out a pro forma profit and loss statement as we have done in Table 4.1. Use costs that you feel could be easily achieved under your own management. This type of profit and loss statement will give you a projected profit that can be called "estimated earning power" under your management. If this figure is more than the present owner is achieving and if you are completely confident that you can do it, then you have an advantage in negotiating a good deal for yourself because the value of the business is heavily influenced by the poorer past performance.

3. *Some Areas Require Your Special Attention.* The cost of goods must be verified. Are raw materials purchased at the best possible prices commensurate with acceptable quality? Check actual invoices. If you are not familiar with average market prices, ask someone who knows. You may uncover an opportunity to reduce the cost of goods or you may find that the owner is using some material that was bought at bargain prices but that is no longer available at those prices. Be especially attentive to large inventories of slow moving items. The cost may be years old.

Check the labor factor in the cost of goods. Is it reasonable? Could you do it cheaper or are the employees underpaid and due for a substantial raise? Be especially watchful for other items charged to the direct cost of goods. Are there any items of direct cost that should be charged to indirect costs or to administrative or selling expense?

When you are satisfied that the cost of goods is fairly represented either in the owner's figures or in your "restructured" figures, compare it with the net sales figure. If the direct cost of goods is high (over 35%) in relation to sales, you may have an unacceptably small margin for error and profit. In other words, the higher the direct cost of goods (labor and material) in relation to net sales, the less money there is for indirect administrative and selling expense and, of course, earnings. This ratio of direct costs to sales, in a sense, determines where your attention will be directed if you buy the business. If you are the seller, you must have your house in order if you are going to close a successful deal with a knowledgeable buyer.

For the buyer a high cost of goods requires a very tight control of the manufacturing end of the business. If the cost of goods is low, you will probably be spending more of your time on administrative and selling problems.

All manufacturing expenses not directly associated with the products can be considered indirect and are somewhat more controllable than the direct expenses of labor and material. These indirect expenses consist of such items as factory rent, light, heat, supervisory wages, supplies, and maintenance. They should be examined closely to determine if there is any room for improvement or if they are unrealistically low.

Administrative expense generally covers clerical functions (processing orders, handling correspondence and telephone, maintaining files, etc.), bookkeeping, and general management. In a very small company where the owner handles production, administration, and sales activities, his compensation should be proportionately distributed to all of these activities; however, this method is seldom used and you must take this inaccuracy into account in the evaluation of expenses.

Administrative expenses are where to look for relatives on the payroll. They may be performing a useful function or they may be "advisory."

Although many small businesses today still use the term *selling expense* to describe a section in their profit and loss statement, the secret of success or reason for failure of a small business is often found in its "marketing activities," which should include a lot more than selling. This area requires your most diligent attention because here you will generally find the true indication of the earning power of an enterprise.

If your "restructured" financial statements indicate that the business has low earning power, look at the marketing activities for clues as to why the owner has failed to produce satisfactory earnings and how you can improve them.

Some of the important aspects of marketing that were mentioned in the preliminary analysis and require a closer look include:

1. Does the owner have a detailed, carefully-thought-out annual marketing plan with clearly defined objectives and ways and means to achieve these objectives? Or does he or she say "this business could be a real gold mine if I wanted to do a little advertising."

2. Is the sales literature up-to-date and of good quality? Don't forget the cost of reprinting or developing new literature in your restructured profit and loss statement.

3. Does the company have an aggressive advertising program with attractive ads and the services of a good advertising agency?

4. Are sales inquiries sought and properly handled?

5. Does the owner have any method for measuring the effectiveness of advertising?

6. Is there any market research? Does the owner have an intimate knowledge of current markets? Are there plans for developing new markets?

7. How much does the owner spend on marketing? How much should be spent? How much would you spend if you owned the business?

If the marketing costs and manufacturing expenses seem to be reasonable, you cannot improve the earnings unless you can increase sales. This requires a good knowledge of the market. If you do not have this knowledge, you generally acquire it within a year or so.

Most prospects for buying small manufacturing companies today generally search for opportunities that are familiar to them, where they know the technology or the markets and they have lots of ideas on making or selling the products. However, it is amazing how many small business owners do not have any idea of the size or character of their markets and, worse, have no idea how to find out.

WHAT IS THE CASH FLOW?

You've got to have cash with which to buy materials and services, pay wages, taxes and interest, maintain your building and machinery, and you should plan on keeping some in the bank for emergencies. Can the business generate all the cash you need from the first day you own the company? Check by doing a simple cash flow analysis, as shown in Table 4.3.

Using a conservative pro forma profit and loss statement, make an estimate of monthly cash expenses and cash income. Use the monthly sales figures from the previous year as a basis for estimating the pro forma sales figures. In the example, this analysis shows a cash need of about $19,000 if sales were fairly level. Things almost never work out exactly in this type of cash flow projection, and it would be wise to figure on at least $25,000 cash need.

WHAT ARE THE ASSETS REALLY WORTH?

Fair market value was defined in the Preface, however, this term must be interpreted carefully, taking the circumstances of both the buyer and the seller into account. Many small business owners don't know the value of their business and therefore might ask an unreasonably high price, or they might be persuaded to sell at a lower price than should be expected. Some buyers might place a higher value on the business than the owner does because the earnings (or losses) would produce tax advantages for the buyer that the seller doesn't know about. Other prospective buyers may place too high a value on the business due to ignorance, lack of experience, or poor advice.

The best way for a small business owner to determine the current market value of the business is to have it appraised by a professional business appraiser. Another way to determine its value is to solicit offers from serious and knowledgeable prospects. To get the best offer, the owner should do everything possible to make the situation attractive.

HOW CAN VALUES BE ASSIGNED TO ASSETS?

During your contacts with the owners of small manufacturing companies that are for sale, you may have a difficult time trying to get an owner to put an asking price on the business (in most cases it is to your benefit to buy only productive assets). As mentioned previously, the owner probably doesn't know how to value the assets and may be trying to get a free appraisal of the business from you.

If you are a sophisticated and knowledgeable but disinterested businessperson, your appraisal of the business might be a good measure of "fair market value." However, you are not a disinterested appraiser—you are a prospective buyer and you want to buy the business for the lowest possible price. Furthermore, you do not initially want to reveal the value you place on the assets but simply make an offer that may be less than you think the business is worth. If the owner thinks that your offer is too low, you may wish to convince him or her of its validity by indicating how you value the assets.

The assets of a small manufacturing company are generally these:

Physical or Tangible Assets

1. Land and buildings
2. Machinery and equipment
3. Inventory
4. Accounts receivable, cash, securities

Intangible Assets

1. Goodwill (earning power)
2. Skills and knowledge of the owner and employees (know-how)
3. Patents, trade secrets, trademarks

For the exercise of assigning values to the assets, see Chapter 4. If you cannot make a reasonable estimate you will have to get help—preferably from experts, but a well-informed friend may be able to help you.

Initially you have to take the word of the seller on the value of the inventory (which is often higher than that shown on the balance sheet). However, it should be checked later in great detail (and your offer adjusted accordingly) to determine how it is valued and if it is all correct, in first-class condition, and balanced. If you discover a three-month supply of one part and a five-year supply of another, the inventory is unbalanced, and anything over a year's supply (less in some cases) should be valued lower than the first year's supply. In a product line where changes and improvements take place frequently, a five-year supply of parts might be 75% worthless. On the other hand a five-year supply of some common part like nuts and bolts might be greatly undervalued.

Assuming you have made the calculations described in Table 4.2, and have assigned values to the assets, put yourself in the position of the seller. What values do you think he or she might assign to the individual assets? How should he or she react to your values?

Now decide what kind of an offer would be appropriate to interest the seller enough to consider you a serious prospect. Your objective now, if you want to close a deal, is to keep negotiations going.

HOW TO EVALUATE THE OWNER'S COMPENSATION

In any closely held company the compensation of the owner/stockholders must be examined very carefully. This compensation often does not reflect the true value of their services. You will find an extreme range of personal whims, fancies, and occasionally logical reasons why the owner/stockholder compensation is what it is. Here are a few things to look for:

1. Often the owner of a small business assumes unbelievable responsibilities: chief executive, sales manager, production manager, treasurer, and janitor. And the owner may feel (and the IRS may agree) that he or she is entitled to

two or three full salaries. When you see very high individual compensation, you should remember that a jack-of-all-trades often does the work of two or three people.

2. Look for fringe benefits that may not be appropriate or required under new ownership: exorbitant car and travel expenses, pension plans, life insurance, high costs of trade shows, conventions, seminars, entertainment, sales meetings, especially those in resort areas and foreign countries. A $4,000 trip to Europe for the chief executive of a small manufacturing company with sales of $250,000 per year may be allowed as a deductible expense by the IRS, but it is probably not essential to the welfare of the company.

3. Watch out for very low owner compensation. He or she may be grossly underpaid because the business is inefficient and unable to pay a decent salary—or the owner might be taking a low salary in order to make the company earnings look better.

4. Check the balance sheet for loans to officers and officer loans to the company. The circumstances behind these loans often reveal valuable information for evaluation of the company's operations.

Evaluating the opportunity accurately is a vital element of success for both the seller and the buyer. If the deal fails, the seller has to take back the business or the bank gets it and the buyer loses both shirt and reputation. The only winners are the lawyers and the vultures.

9

Corporate Acquisitions

As discussed in Chapter 1, expansion by acquisition is an expedient way for a small manufacturer to grow and diversify. This route, however, requires a special strategy that has to be developed by the corporate buyer, preferably by the chief executive officer. It is very risky to acquire small companies without a carefully thought-out plan not only for the search and acquisition phase but more importantly for the operational and developmental phase.

Adding sales volume by acquisition of other small companies is an acceptable way to grow, but the acquisitions will not be satisfying if they dilute earnings for the sake of volume. They must contribute to the growth of earnings as well as volume. It is not necessary that the growth in volume of the new acquisitions be the only source of additional earnings. Incremental earnings can be generated by cost reductions in the new acquisition. The main source of cost reduction will often be in reduced management expense.

In the case of the corporate buyer, the strategy for success must include the middle management of the buying company. Every acquisition that we have ever made has always been a team effort with important roles specifically assigned to middle managers. This strategy requires considerable preparation and training, at least for the first corporate acquisition. On the second or third acquisition your team operates much more effectively and by the fourth or fifth you have an enthusiastic group of experienced professionals.

Careful selection of the acquisition team should take place before a prospect has been targeted. Training sessions should include a review of the corporate acquisition objectives and the techniques by which prospects are developed. Middle managers should participate in this phase of the acquisitions and should be required to find or suggest suitable prospects. In addition to developing enthusiastic and loyal managers, you also enrich their careers, especially when you lay on the responsibility and authority for important acquisition planning and decisions.

In some cases an acquisition will be such an important segment of your business that you will need a major division manager. The risk is less if you already have a proven manager who you can put in charge of the new acquisition. This option provides a challenge to the manager not only to succeed at a new and interesting opportunity but to select and train his or her own replacement. If you are lucky enough to get a good manager with the acquisition, have him or her report to one of your own executives. In this way your new manager learns the management policies and practices in your company.

It is important to include as many of your employees as possible in the new acquisition program. Get all the officers and top managers of your company involved, and any that may be coming with the acquisition, as well as the foremen, clerks, and secretaries who will have to help with new administrative and operational duties.

Be sure that there is a checklist of everything that has to be done and who is responsible for doing it, from designing and printing new stationery, labels, and product name plates to marketing plans, financial projections, accounting procedures, and management controls.

The many advantages of small corporate acquisitions include two essential elements of success that are often neglected by entrepreneurs: management training and synergism. Too few small companies pay much attention to management development. Owners complain that their employees are too busy to devote any significant time to training. These same owners will often evaluate an acquisition prospect on the basis of problems only without regard for the synergistic opportunities. Both of these essential elements are worthy of special attention.

TRAINING

In all phases of your business, people are the key to success and you cannot execute a systematic acquisition program unless you have an enthusiastic management team. This may sound like a difficult thing to achieve in a small company where owner/managers are expected to be all things to all people but it can be done. We have developed a training program that we call the "closed-loop case method" which works well in developing acquisition analysis skills among our managers. This program was described in an article by the author in the July–August 1985 issue of the *Harvard Business Review* (see Appendix D).

Briefly, the closed-loop case method involves the use of actual acquisition prospects. The analysis of the prospect is conducted as an in-house case study involving all of our key managers.

The case is written up by one of our top executives following the procedures and guidelines suggested in this book for the buyer (see Chapter 4). Every member of the acquisition team receives a copy of the case and it is discussed in the training sessions. Most members of the team visit the target company when negotiations are under way.

The only difference between this case study as taught in business schools and as used in our company is that our class actually buys a company and is responsible for its successful operation. Our experience indicates that these key managers not only perform well in helping with the acquisition but they become more productive in their regularly assigned duties.

SYNERGISM

Synergism is defined as "the action of two or more substances or organisms to achieve an effect of which each is incapable." Combining two or more small manufacturing entities can produce all kinds of benefits that might be impossible or very difficult to produce independently, such as:

1. A significant reduction of management expense
2. An infusion of new ideas
3. A possible reduction in manufacturing, selling, and administrative expense
4. An enrichment of challenges for middle managers

5. The possible acquisition of outstanding human resources

6. Unused or underused assets such as land, buildings, machinery, and equipment

7. A sudden but easily managed increase in sales volume and cash flow

8. A possible tax benefit if one of the companies is in a temporary loss mode

9. An entry into new markets

10. Geographical diversification of sales and/or manufacturing

Any one of these advantages ought to develop some interest if not outright enthusiasm in a small company owner striving to grow. Here's how they could work for you:

Management

Two small companies, when combined, do not need two presidents, two vice presidents, two treasurers, two personnel managers, or two controllers. Our experience suggests that all management activities down to (but not including) salespeople and foremen can be easily handled by the acquiring company. In many cases this reduces the payroll of the acquired company by 50%. In the case of a poorly managed target company, you not only have the advantage of reduced management expense but the benefit of superior management skills in the acquiring company.

New Ideas

The acquisition of a well-managed company with a long history of success is bound to reveal management practices and ideas that you may find valuable. You may even want to retain the services of the former owner/managers as directors or advisors.

Expense Reduction

Management expense reduction is virtually guaranteed in any prudent small corporate acquisition. Other expense reductions are not so obvious. However, it is reasonable to assume that similar manufacturing operations can be combined, purchasing can be improved, sales administration and order processing can probably be integrated into your operations, and advertising and sales promotion can frequently be absorbed into your existing system. Packaging, shipping, receiving, and inventory control can easily be combined.

These expense improvements are maximized if you can move the new acquisition into the same physical facility (or very nearby) that houses your existing company. In most cases, adding space to your present factory is justified by the advantage of having everything under one roof. We enlarged our factory and offices for every acquisition we made and moved the acquired companies to the central location. Our building grew in a carefully planned manner from 5,000 to 40,000 square feet. We estimate that we save at least $100,000 per year in having all of our companies (five of them) under one roof.

Challenge

For a small manufacturing company to acquire another manufacturing company is an unusual and challenging experience. It is a great opportunity for your middle managers to improve and broaden their skills. For those managers who have some reservations about participating in company acquisitions, a certain amount of training may be required (see Appendix D). However, once you show your managers how they can participate effectively they will give you enthusiastic cooperation.

For some managers a minor role may be best for their first experience, such as the logistics of moving the new acquisition, the plan for space and facilities, an analysis of administrative requirements, or even such details as forms, literature, and letterheads.

A successful acquisition engenders a very positive team spirit and a real sense of creative participation among your managers.

New Talent

One of the first things you should look at in an acquisition prospect is the quality and availability of people in the target company. Who is going to be available? Who would you like to have? Are there any talented potential managers for your own operations as well as the acquired operation?

Most sellers are anxious to see their loyal employees well taken care of. They will eagerly point out their favorites (who may or may not fit into your plans). Some of the most talented employees may consider the sale of their employer to be an opportunity to change jobs, especially if they get a handsome severance payment. If they might be an asset to your organization, you must persuade them that the best opportunities are in staying with the company. One of our best sales managers today came to us with an acquisition.

Underutilized Assets

When you intend to move an acquired manufacturing operation, do not acquire its real estate assets unless they are an
especially good bargain and can be quickly sold or rented.
However, if you see immediate benefits in acquiring real
estate, then consider important longer-range benefits, such
as:

Full utilization of idle or infrequently used machinery.
Could this machinery be used to provide goods and
services for your other companies that are now being
purchased from independent suppliers? Could it be the
basis for a subcontract business to supply other users?

Extra manufacturing space in which to locate some of your
operations now housed in the headquarters building.
For example, if you have machining operations now at
the headquarters location and you acquire another company that also has machining operations, could they be
combined in the new location? This type of integration
might also apply to service or repair facilities, order
processing, or other administrative functions.

If your acquisition program has already resulted in the
purchase of several other companies or product lines,
you may have noted that growth beyond annual sales
of $5 to $10,000,000 required a new layer of staff
managers and administrative overhead is suddenly
accelerating. This is the time to consider a new profit
center and the new acquisition might be the ideal
nucleus for an entirely separate, wholly owned subsidiary—which, in effect, starts a new enterprise in the
same pattern that brought your current company to the
pinnacle of success. At this point your strategy must
change from the single-purpose company that you put

together several years ago. If you are getting good management and real estate that has expansion potential in your newest acquisition, think about letting it operate independently and absorb other acquisitions that you make in the future.

Increased Sales Volume

Traditionally sales volume is increased by achieving a greater market share, creating new markets, or bringing out new products. This goal is generally reached at considerable expense and risk and over a relatively long period of time. The easier, quicker, and less risky route is to acquire a company the sales and profits of which accrue to your company the day you take title to the assets. Not only do you achieve an instant volume increase but hopefully you have as good or better profitability and cash flow than the former owner. If the sales volume of the target company is commensurate with its resources, there is no reason to assume that you will have any serious problems integrating the operation into your own.

Tax Benefits

If your company has been highly successful and is paying maximum income taxes, an acquisition in a temporary loss mode might shelter some of your corporate income. Or, on the contrary, if you are building up annoying carry-forward losses, you should certainly be looking at prospects with a pretty good record of earnings.

There are other tax considerations in depreciable assets that can generally be written up and used to improve cash flow. Another tax advantage still exists for those companies that have significant export business. Export sales are still subsidized by the U.S. government under the new tax laws with special export corporations. As long as the U.S. balance of payments is so disadvantageous, there will be export incentives.

New Markets

Developing new markets from scratch is a laborious chore for small manufacturing companies, especially those in low-technology industries. The acquisition of a company serving the markets you wish to be in is a relatively easy way to penetrate new markets. You can look for prospects who serve a different segment of your present market or you can try to find an acquisition serving a completely different market where your current products are not now sold, but could be sold. For example, a tool that you make for the original equipment manufacturer (OEM) market might have considerable potential in the mail-order market or the do-it-yourself (DIY) market.

Geographical Diversification

There's nothing more gratifying to a marketing manager than having regular sales in every important population center in the world. Although this spread is virtually unachievable for a small manufacturing company, most such manufacturers can certainly have much wider distribution of their products than they now enjoy. If a market-oriented company wants to get into some new market areas quickly, acquisitions could be the right route.

Ten years ago one of our acquisitions was an old manufacturer of a highly competitive consumer hardware product that was sold in only 15 states in the United States. The large and strong competitors had over 90% of the market. By using the mail-order expertise of a previously acquired company, we were able not only to increase market share of the new acquisition but to establish significant sales in all 50 states. These sales have increased every year since the acquisition.

For a successful small manufacturing company, carefully chosen acquisitions can be more fun than the original enterprise.

10

Advice and Assistance

Many successful small business ventures are started by groups of people who are brought together by a common interest, by association in routine relationships, or by chance. Advisors or potential partners in a business will be found most often among trusted associates and professionals.

You will always find a great deal of interest in a new business venture among successful people who are looking for a new challenge and who may have access to capital. A group of talented people are generally more attractive to capital sources than a single individual: The number spreads the risk. Furthermore, the experience of a group is often more than the sum of the individual experiences: Partners serve not only as checks and balances on each other but as movers and shakers of ideas.

Whether you are a partner in a group or an individual with advisors, you have to find opportunities, develop plans, negotiate a deal, get financing, and operate the enterprise. You need expertise in law, accounting, financing, and operations, so you turn to lawyers, accountants, bankers (or investors), managers, and maybe partners.

LAWYERS

Although lawyers generally do not show great interest in being entrepreneurs, they are indispensable professionals in business law. No entrepreneur should ever embark on any business venture or enter into any agreement or contract without the advice and counsel of a lawyer skilled in business law. As indicated in Chapter 4, a lawyer can be a good source of acquisition prospects and those who have manufacturing clients are those you should be meeting. If you do not have a good working relationship with a lawyer, establish one. Lawyers should not be brought into a deal until negotiations are well underway and there is a verbal agreement in principle between the buyer and the seller. My experience has been that lawyers do not think the way entrepreneurs do and sometimes have no idea of values when it comes to judging the potential of a small manufacturing enterprise.

Accountants

All significant asset owners (individual or corporate) have accountants who figure out profit or loss, net worth, taxes, depreciation, and other accounting matters and arrange all of the figures in a systematic and useful manner. Accounting is often a weakness of entrepreneurs, but they should learn to recognize the importance and value of tight fiscal controls as a management tool.

Both buyers and sellers of businesses should get together with their accountants as early as possible (after financial information has been exchanged but well before any negotiations take place) to discuss the "balance sheet" strategy.

Although accountants, like lawyers, may not have good value judgment in analyzing the potential of a small manufacturing company, they can certainly interpret the numbers. No financial information of any kind should escape their perusal—including the seller's roughest estimates of costs, profit and loss, net worth, and debt to equity. If you are the seller, you may need certified financial statements with an accountant's verification of inventory. Unaudited financial statements cast serious doubts on the value of a manufacturing business.

FINANCE SOURCES

Debt and equity capital are often represented by different types of people or institutions. The entrepreneur will almost always be an equity participant and often a lender. Conventional banks are lenders but seldom owners (except by default). Venture capitalists or individual investors will want a piece of the action (equity).

In any venture where you need financial resources other than your own, you will usually find yourself both a stockholder and a bond or note holder (secured or unsecured). It always makes good sense to be not only compatible with your fellow investors but cordial and even downright friendly. At times mutual trust and friendship are the only glue that holds an enterprise together.

As soon as you start talking to a prospective seller, you should be talking to prospective investors. Even if you don't need outside capital, you should use a little just to establish relationships with fellow investors. The old saying that banks loan money only to people who don't need it really means that financial institutions depend on successful entrepreneurs to help keep the money circulating.

In addition to being a source of financing, investors (especially venture capitalists) are valuable advisors, often with direct experience in the type of business you are buying. They also have constant access to opportunities suitable for your business, such as potential acquisitions, talented personnel, and export connections.

Most sellers of businesses have long-standing financial advisors and don't need any further help. But many buyers are first-time investors who have had few significant relationships with banks and perhaps no experience at all with venture capital or partners. This may be the most critical hurdle in buying a small manufacturing company. It pays to handle it with great care.

Other Small Business Owners

Many people have become entrepreneurs by talking with successful small business owners. Entrepreneurism is infectious. Just ask any happy owner of a small company to tell you about his or her business.

If you don't know any owners of small manufacturing businesses, try to meet some. One of the most favorable avenues is to go to meetings and seminars held for small businesses. Organizations of small business owner/managers are found in almost every major population center in the United States.

We have belonged to the Small Business Association of New England for 25 years and have met hundreds of owners and managers who represent a typical cross-section of American small business enterprise, all the way from $50,000 to $50,000,000 in annual sales. Their collective experience is a rich resource for facing every conceivable problem and opportunity that a small company might have.

Small business associations often publish membership directories and newsletters. These are available for the asking. The size of businesses is indicated in other standard directories, such as Thomas Register, McCrae's, and Dun & Bradstreet. Mailing lists are available from the list publishers for small businesses by product or geographical location. Chambers of commerce in large cities will have a directory identifying small businesses in that area.

You can also meet successful business owners in community organizations such as clubs, churches, PTAs and college alumni organizations.

Key Employees

Andrew Carnegie attributed his success to hiring managers who were smarter than he was. However, an entrepreneur like Carnegie is unlikely to be the least talented person on a management team. He probably meant that he hired people who had superior abilities in certain areas that complemented rather than dominated others. In any event, the most successful companies tend to have above-average human resources and here is where you must look for the real strength of an organization. You must be able to recognize latent ability, develop it through leadership and training, and then use it.

In the search for and evaluation of acquisition opportunities, you will often find valuable information among the middle management sector of the target company. If you find a dearth of talent there or ineffective use of talent, your prospects for improving the company are greater.

Often the owner/manager of a small company is a strong, dominating, and sometimes intolerant person who will not share responsibility and authority. He or she won't hire ambitious and talented managers for fear of losing control. He or she lacks important leadership qualities that distinguish the successful entrepreneur from the not-so-successful.

The attitudes and thoughts of middle managers are often a reflection of the character of a company and can frequently reveal more about operations than do extended conversations with the owner/manager. Don't overlook this valuable source of intelligence.

TRADE ASSOCIATIONS

Trade associations exist for almost every industry from peanut growers and morticians to steel makers and aircraft manufacturers. These associations protect and promote the special interests of the industry and you can get all kinds of information by contacting an industry's trade association. Look for directories of these associations in public libraries and also examine the directories of trade publications (*Standard Rate & Data* published by Standard Rate & Data Service, Inc, 3004 Glenview Road, Wilmette, Illinois 60091).

Lots of areas should be checked if you are buying a manufacturing company in an industry with which you have not had much experience. For example, the industry may use toxic chemicals, which could pose work place or environmental problems. The company may have a high incidence of product liability exposure. There may be severe foreign competition. The industry may also present unusual opportunities for the innovative entrepreneur who is looking for challenges. Plenty of industries in the United States are in trouble and need new ideas.

FRIENDS AND RELATIVES

Friends and relatives are a risky source of advice and assistance unless a very special relationship exists between you. Their trust is generally based on a personal relationship rather than on an analytical appraisal of you and the target company and their advice could result in awkward or embarrassing situations. In some cases, misunderstandings are so acute that the business fails, law suits are instigated, life-long friendships are destroyed, or, even worse, mayhem and bodily injuries are inflicted.

Needless to say, getting advice and assistance from friends and relatives is a highly personal matter and the only comment that can be made by a disinterested party is "good luck."

11

Negotiations

In Chapters 8 and 10 we discussed the valuation of the target company and sources of advice and assistance. Assuming that you have selected your first target company, done your evaluation carefully, and reviewed it with your advisors, you are now ready to start negotiations.

By now you should have had several meetings with the seller and should have an idea of the value he or she has placed on the business. Perhaps the seller has given you a range of values depending on what assets you buy or a firm price for the stock of the corporation. In all probability your and the seller's value judgments will vary considerably. Your ability to reduce this variance will be a test of your entrepreneurial skills.

When you have reached the negotiation stage of an acquisition you have probably decided that you, as the buyer, want to acquire the target company and the owner wants to sell it to you. However the seller is asking for more than what you think the company is worth or, in the seller's view, you are offering less than what he or she expected. How do you preceed with the negotiations?

NEGOTIABLE ALTERNATIVES

If you really like the opportunity, if you feel that you can be very successful, and if you have protected yourself with a safe margin for error and slippage, then develop several realistic alternatives for presentation to the seller. In estimating the situation you have to assume the following conditions that the seller will probably not discuss with you (and you may lose the deal if you ask):

1. *The Seller's Financial Condition.* Does he or she need cash desperately? Is he or she in big trouble? Or is the seller very liquid with a high net worth and capable of holding onto the business indefinitely?

2. *Key Employees.* Is the owner about to lose a vitally important key employee who will become a competitor? Are the key employees happy or upset at the prospect of a new owner?

3. *Health.* Are any of the owners, managers, or key employees in poor health or very anxious to retire?

4. *Major Customers.* Are any major customers in trouble or about to change ownership? If the seller lets you talk to them, fine. If not, look out.

5. *Hidden Liabilities.* Buying only assets will relieve you of some hidden liabilities (not all of them). However, product liability for past sins sometimes is passed on to

a successor corporation regardless of "hold harmless" clauses in contracts. There is some risk here that you cannot avoid.

In your estimate of the situation a variety of alternate terms and conditions could be the key to success. If a seller's firm price demand seems entirely out of line, you will have to decide if any other prospective buyer might pay it under terms and conditions set by the seller.

If the price seems too high but the seller's terms are negotiable, there may be plenty of opportunities to work something out. For example:

Offer to pay for a noncompete agreement (a deductible expense for a buyer)

Offer a percentage of profit or sales incentive paid only if the business does as well as the seller claims it can do

Let the seller keep the real estate and pay him or her rent (depreciation deductible by seller)

Give the seller a consulting contract (deductible expense to you)

Ask the seller to finance some of the purchase price at a rate below market

Your pro forma profit and loss statements should indicate a range of values that are documented and can be justified on a line-by-line basis. If you've done your homework well, you have identified each item of expense that is more or less than you think it should be. These variances can be explained to the seller to justify the values you have established. For example, let us assume that a new catalog has to be designed and printed. It will cost $10,000. That cost goes into your first year's pro forma operating expense. Let us further assume that there have been no wage increases in the company for two years. You feel that a 10% increase is imperative in your first year. You add this to your pro forma expense.

These types of increased expenses are obvious and cannot be denied. Potential cost savings are less obvious. Perhaps you can buy some materials cheaper, maybe you could redesign the product to reduce cost, or you might install some labor-saving methods or machines. Cost increases, however, generally come quicker than cost savings. The seller will argue that there are lots of ways to reduce costs, but remember: If the seller hasn't found a way, you might not be able to either.

Capitalized values of earnings at various levels of sales are good illustrations of a range of values of the business that you can document, as illustrated in Chapter 4. Use these figures to justify to the seller the validity of your values. He or she cannot deny that your goal of a 10% return in the investment is extremely modest.

INITIAL PROPOSAL

Your initial proposal should be based on your real feelings about the company and how well you think you can run it. If this impression requires a higher price than you had expected to offer, you should negotiate aggressively on terms. Favorable terms can be better than a lower price in many cases.

The greatest challenge for the buyer at the proposal stage is to convince the seller that he or she is the best prospect. The buyer must impress the seller with knowledge and skills in all aspects of the business. If there are any payments contingent on the future success of the business, the buyer must certainly convince the seller that he or she can run the business as well as or better than the seller.

It is important to the buyer to be able to judge correctly the true motivation of the seller in offering the business for sale. Has the seller lost confidence in the future or in his or her own ability to cope with an increasingly complex and frustrating business environment? Has the seller become bored and eager to do something else? Is a health problem the catalyst? Does the seller have a personal problem: family, financial, or legal?

For any obviously serious problems with the business, the owner will invariably offer rationalizations such as: "I've been spending too much time on the golf course," "I stopped advertising," "I haven't had a new catalog in five years," "I lost my best foreman," or "I made a bad mistake but it can be easily corrected." The hidden problems may not be revealed by these excuses and it's the buyer's responsibility to study the situation carefully enough to see causal relationships. For example, there may be a new technology that seriously threatens the future of the business, there may be a new strong competitor coming into the industry, or there may be serious product obsolescence problems that are not yet apparent.

The seller must likewise figure out the buyer's motivation. If the seller has a long history of profitability, is the buyer looking primarily for a tax offset to past losses carried forward? If so, the business may be worth more to the tax loss buyer than to other prospects. Is the buyer going to liquidate the business, or merge it into another business? Is he or she going to move the operations? Will he or she be able to pay all on-going obligations to the seller? Will the seller be getting large amounts of ordinary income instead of capital gains? Will the seller end up in tax court?

PERSONALITIES

In any negotiations, the personalities of the negotiators play a significant role in the results. Both buyers and sellers of manufacturing businesses tend to have strong, domineering personalities and therein lies a potential problem. Many deals have fallen apart because of personality clashes: The seller is insulted by what he or she thinks is a ridiculous and frivolous offer, the buyer can be offended by a seller's outrageously high asking price. You must remember that the initial values put on the businesses by interested parties are "exploratory" and should be used only as a reference point. I have seen a business sold for $300,000 for which the initial asking price was $2 million. I've also seen a business professionally appraised at a fair market value of $1 million go for more than $3 million. These wide variations in perceived and actual values were probably the result of personality differences of the negotiators rather than errors in judging value.

A certain amount of seller's "puffery" or "blue sky" should be expected in any deal and an equal amount of uncertainty and downside risk will be introduced by the prospective buyer.

THREE FINANCIAL ROUTES

The seller's financial condition (which will probably not be revealed to a buyer) and the buyer's financial strength often determine the financial structure of the deal. If the credit of the buyer is questionable or the seller is hurting for cash, the seller may insist on all cash up front (at closing or very soon thereafter). The all-cash deal is the easiest route for negotiating discounts.

The most common route is some cash down with the balance scheduled in accordance with the cash flow of the business plus the assets of the buyer.

The best deal for the buyer is little or no cash down with scheduled payments out of cash flow of the business (leveraged buy out) in which the seller finances the entire transaction. This deal is most common with very financially strong buyers who may pledge assets other than those of the target business and who can guarantee payment regardless of the outcome of the business.

For a financially weak buyer who must come up with all the cash at the closing, the best bet is probably a partner. Such a buyer will be lucky to retain control of the company. Large investors like to have control and, of course, ultimate control is on the "wish list" of small investors. But if you do not possess significant financial strength, you have to be patient and make more deals.

When Royal Little was putting Narragansett Capital together, he frequently gave the sellers, managers, or owners (who went with the businesses sold to Narragansett) a generous "piece of the action" and often an option to get more. The greatest work incentive in the world is ownership control.

The success or failure of negotiations in buying and selling a small manufacturing business to a large extent is determined by the abilities of both the buyer and the seller. These abilities are developed through experience. No other way to learn is better than face-to-face encounters in real situations.

12

Financing

The three financial routes introduced in Chapter 11 were:

1. All cash at closing with probable immediate tax liability for the seller.
2. Twenty-nine percent down (30% or less qualifies as an installment sale), balance in regular installments with seller paying taxes on the installments.
3. Little cash down, balance out of earnings.

The funds for any of these transactions can come from a variety of sources: the buyer's own capital; capital borrowed by the buyer from friends, relatives, banks, insurance companies, venture capitalists, private investors, or other financial institutions; equity capital contributed by investors other than the buyer; or earnings of the enterprise.

119

There are many other ways in which asset ownership can be transferred: It can be exchanged for other physical assets such as machinery, real estate, or aircraft, or for nonphysical assets such as securities, notes, and services. It can also be transferred by will or gift. We will limit our discussion, however, to the most common means of transferring title.

CASH AT CLOSING

If you are convinced that the return on investment in the target company can be 20% or more under your leadership, you might want to consider liquidating investments that are yielding less than 20% and putting them into the target company. There are some advantages in providing 100% of the purchase price from your own resources. First, you do not have to negotiate and meet the terms, conditions, or whims of any other person or institution except the seller's. You are under no obligation to pay any loans and you start off your new business with a very strong balance sheet, providing you don't assume any significant liabilities of the seller. Banks are favorably inclined to make very competitive working capital loans to companies with strong balance sheets and generous capital contributions of confident owners.

Another advantage of cash at closing is a strong bargaining position. Many sellers like prospects who offer cash up front and they will often grant a generous cash discount. You may close the deal at 5 or 10% less than your competitor who offers a low down payment and extended term or terms contingent upon sales or profits.

There is also the advantage of more cash flow in the business if you do not have high interest and principal payments in debt. If the business needs cash flow for growth and you don't feel comfortable with heavy debt, put your assets in your own business.

INSTALLMENT SALE

An installment sale is partially financed by a seller who has a great deal of faith in the buyer. In an installment sale the seller generally holds a mortgage on the assets and regains title to the assets if the buyer defaults. However, the seller has then not achieved the goal of selling the company and may recover a picked-clean skeleton of the business that will probably be worth less than the amount still owing at default. This outcome is common enough to create a great deal of stress for both the buyer and the seller.

As a seller, don't do an installment deal unless you are absolutely convinced of the buyer's ability to be successful.

CONDITIONAL SALE

An arrangement whereby the seller finances the whole deal in exchange for a performance sweetener can sometimes be advantageous for both parties. If the buyer is successful and is able to increase sales and earnings more than projected, the seller gets more than he or she expected and the buyer also benefits. However, there is a great risk in this type of arrangement and a lot of the details are not mutually controllable. This type of sale is probably best reserved for intrafamily transfers where filial relationships take precedence over purely objective decisions.

PAYOUT FROM EARNINGS

Although leveraged buyouts depend on a reliable flow of earnings, deals can be structured in which the seller assumes some of the risk by agreeing to take part payment out of "surplus earnings." If the company has a long history of predictable earnings and the seller feels confident that the buyer will not only maintain this momentum but improve earnings, the seller can agree to share any surplus earnings over and above the base contract price. This arrangement is essentially a profit-sharing plan.

In this type of deal it is assumed that the base price for the business is somewhat less than the seller expected but the profit share, if realized, would put the total paid by the buyer at a greater amount than the seller expected.

The problem is that it is difficult to define the trigger point profit. The buyer has the right to make expenditures and raise wages and salaries in such ways as to always remain below the profit trigger point. Of course, you could make the profit share a function of shipments, but these too can be manipulated by someone acting in bad faith. Or perfectly legitimate fluctuations in the normal course of events can ruin the deal for a seller.

I have seen profit-sharing work extremely well in some cases and very poorly in others, but it always has a high risk factor.

LEVERAGED LIQUIDITY

Many owners of successful small manufacturing companies, after they have passed the critical start-up or new owner phase, find that most of their personal or family net worth is represented by the equity in their company. As the company continues to grow, its need for capital increases. Although growth capital is readily available for successful small companies, some owners take pride in financing their growth solely out of earnings. There is generally nothing wrong with this conservative business philosophy, but it might result in liquidity problems and require a slowdown in growth.

For owners who are illiquid but are not yet ready to cash in all of their chips, there is an interesting way to achieve liquidity and still retain a generous piece of the equity. I call it "leveraged liquidity." It also goes by the term *disproportionate partial redemption* or *leveraged recapitalization* (used by the venture capital group of Bankers Trust Company).

Leveraged liquidity is most commonly applied to companies with annual revenues over $10 million and net earnings after tax over $1 million. However, it has been beneficially applied to companies with as little as $3 million in annual sales and earnings of $300,000, and it would probably work on smaller companies with good track records.

The new investor in leveraged liquidity is generally a new company composed of an investor (bank, SBIC, or other regulated financial institution), you (the owner), and your key managers. A bank or SBIC is not only forbidden by law from controlling manufacturing companies but is not interested in control; however, if the investors are individuals or a group of private investors or another manufacturing company, they would not be legally prevented from buying control of the target company. The owner should clearly understand the investor's legal status and intentions.

The object of leveraged liquidity is to provide maximum cash to the owner while still allowing him or her to own a significant part of the business (up to 49% initially),* to continue as chief operating officer, and to have an opportunity (if properly understood) to regain voting control of the company (up to 100% at a later date). Under pre-1987 tax laws such an agreement did not constitute a sale. The 1987 tax reform did not change this.

The steps required to achieve leveraged liquidity are the following:

1. A suitable investor has to be found.

2. A new company (N) is formed for the purpose of "purchasing" the target company (T).

3. The stockholders of the new company (N) are:

    a. The former owner of (T): 49%*

    b. The investor (individual, bank, investor group, SBIC, or another company): 49%

    c. Fulcrum group (probably key executives of (T) or others agreed on by buyer and seller): 2%

4. The debt is refinanced by (N) and generally includes senior bank debt and subordinated notes to the investor.

5. The shell of (T) is liquidated or retained by the owner as a holding company for unsold assets such as land, buildings, and securities.

The profile of the original company (T) and the new restructured company (N) are shown in Table 12.1. The owner's benefits are shown at the end of the example. The buyer (investor) gets 49% of the equity and has anticipated

*Can be more than 49% if (1) the investors are willing, (2) the original ownership is in the hands of two or more people not related through attribution (as defined for tax purposes), or (3) the owner does not insist on capital gains treatment.

TABLE 12.1
Profile of the Target Company (T)

Revenues	$3,000,000
Operating profit	300,000
Interest expense	40,000
Pretax profit	260,000
Tax at 34%*	88,000
	172,000
Current assets	400,000
Fixed	700,000
	1,100,000
Current liabilities	200,000
Long-term debt	400,000
Equity	500,000
	1,100,000

Capitalization of New Company (N)

Bank debt	$1,000,000
Subordinated debt	350,000
Common stock	150,000

Equity

Owner	49%	$ 73,500
Investor	49%	73,500
Fulcrum investors	2%	3,000
		150,000

Owner of (T)

Receives	$1,100,000
Pays tax**	168,000
Invests in (N)	73,500
Net cash taken out	858,500

*The new tax regulations reduce corporate rate from 46% to 34% starting 1 July 1987.

**Figures at 28% on gain that is effective in 1988.

an internal rate of return of 25 to 40% on the investment over a period of 5 to 10 years. Sometimes these deals reach the investor's objectives sooner. Sometimes they never reach the objectives.

The investor will obviously be in a position to monitor management effectiveness but will certainly not interfere, if things go as they have in the past and are expected to go in the future. I serve on the boards of several small manufacturing companies with investor representatives whose experience and counsel is a valuable and inexpensive resource for the management of the company. The fulcrum owners play a critical role in the management of the company. They should be trusted key officers of the company and must be chosen carefully.

When everything works out as planned in a leveraged liquidity deal, all participants benefit substantially. The owner gives up a portion of control (which he or she may be able to recover) in exchange for having net worth in cash; the investor assumes the bulk of the financial risk formerly held by the owner, hopefully in exchange for a handsome return in assuming the risk; and the fulcrum investors get a lot of attention for practically nothing and a worthwhile profit if they perform. In successful leveraged liquidity deals, participants are downright jubilant. However, there are failures, and the risk is not insignificant.

Table 12.1 is an example of how a leveraged liquidity might work in a company with $3 million in annual revenues.

You will note from the example that the owner of (T) has effectively given up 52% of the company for a net price after tax of $858,500. If he performs well in the next five years or so, he has a chance to buy back the 49% from the other investors who are in only for a relatively short-term profit (not control). He probably should leave the minority equity with the key managers who may be prospects to acquire his equity in another leveraged deal.

The leveraged liquidity deal is generally not recommended in a situation where the owner wants to retire immediately or in the near future. The success of the venture depends on the experienced owner remaining with the company long enough for the buyer (investors) to achieve their goals of 25 to 40% internal rate of return. If this is achieved the seller's 49% equity shares in the rewards of success.

As is apparent from the distribution of the reorganized ownership, this situation may not be as attractive a deal for the investor as the acquisition of 100% control (when the investor is not an institution forbidden to own control). However, if the acquired company has a good track record and a high probability of future success, this may be the only way that an aggressive investor can persuade a reluctant seller to consider selling an interest in the company. It nets the owner a disproportionately high cash yield, a substantial equity position, and effective control of the company. Also this is a good way to find out how the financial market values your company.

The success of leveraged liquidity depends to a great extent on the ability of the investor to negotiate the bank financing of the new company. Many sophisticated investors are ready and eager to do this kind of transaction, among them Bankers Trust Capital Corporation.

OTHER TERMS AND CONDITIONS

Noncompete Agreements

The buyer should always try to get the seller to agree to allocating part of the purchase price to a noncompete agreement. This is a deductible expense for the buyer and ordinary income to the seller.

Goodwill

Any premium paid over book value (excluding goodwill) may be allocated to goodwill but generally the fair market value of machinery, equipment, and buildings is considerably greater than the depreciated value at the time of sale. Therefore these values can be written up to current fair market and give the buyer a higher depreciation factor than the seller had. This factor is critical in figuring your pro forma cash flow.

13

Closing the Deal

If negotiations have led to general agreement between the buyer and seller, then it's time to bring in the lawyers, accountants, and bankers.

I like to start this phase of an acquisition with a written statement of understanding and intent, which is a summary of the situation that identifies the areas of agreement, the areas of disagreement with suggestions on how they might be resolved, and other matters that have yet to be clarified. This is not an official or binding document and can be written by the buyer or the seller (or both) for use among their respective associates and advisors. It can also be used to confirm between the buyer and the seller any verbal understandings that may eventually have to be reduced to contractual form. On the document indicate clearly that its purpose is to confirm a serious intent and to be a prelude to a formal agreement.

The letter of intent will be very helpful to the lawyer who has to prepare the contract. It should be formulated several days after a verbal agreement in principle has been reached and after both the buyer and the seller have had a few days to talk with their associates and advisors and to think about the consequences of finalizing the deal.

When you have arrived at the point of "agreement in principle," get your lawyer to make a first draft of the contract. He or she will ask you all kinds of questions, such as:

1. What are you buying and what are you not buying?
2. How much are you paying?
3. What are the terms and conditions of payment?
4. When and where is the closing?
5. Are there any agreements regarding:
   a. Disclosure and competition
   b. Consulting
   c. Contracts with third parties
   d. Inventory
   e. Indemnification
   f. Escape clauses
   g. Broker's or finder's fees

After the draft is typed, review it to see that everything is as you (the buyer) think it should be to be acceptable to the seller. In addition to all of the above information, there will be lots of "boiler plate" (standard contractual statements and conditions) that may be quite unfamiliar to you. But remember that your lawyer now exercises quite a bit of control in this transaction and you should accept his or her advice and counsel, except in purely business matters (such as price or terms) where you cast the final judgment.

In Appendix E you will find an exact copy (names and

figures disguised) of an acquisition agreement for a company that had annual sales of about $100,000 per year. We paid less than $85,000 for the assets, which were generating about $25,000 in pretax profits. Ten years later this acquisition had annual sales of $210,000 with $35,000 of contribution to administrative overhead and profit as a division of a larger unit. Twenty-five years after acquisition sales were $600,000 with a $130,000 contribution.

Although a contract and a closing imply that the deal is done, some matters may not be finalized at closing. For example, the seller may agree to buy all the inventory contingent on its salability within a certain time. If it isn't sold during the agreed-upon time, an adjustment has to be made. Or the seller may agree to take only a one year's supply of inventory with an agreement to take more as soon as the initial stock is sold.

The handling of receivables has to be worked out. This is generally done by identifying the orders that become the seller's receivables and must be paid to the seller if and when received. Sometimes the buyer gets the receivables, in which case he or she must collect them and assume the credit risk.

During the "shake-down" period, the buyer confers with the seller about policy and procedure, occasionally about technical matters, and frequently on special situations that may not have been covered during negotiations. It is very much to the mutual benefit of the buyer and the seller to maintain cordial, even friendly relations throughout the negotiations and for a considerable period thereafter. Most sellers enjoy being asked for advice by buyers. In our experience, a friendly seller is extremely important to the buyer during the first year of new ownership.

The buying and selling of a small manufacturing company will produce profound effects on both the seller and the buyer if they are individuals. Think about it:

Thoughts of the Seller	Thoughts of the Buyer
No more authority or responsibility for the assets	New responsibilities and opportunities
A lot of cash to manage	Cash needed to run the business and pay the seller
May be out of a job	Immediate new challenge
Familiar places and faces gone	New relationships and people to get to know
No more selling	New marketing plans to be developed
Can I be an advisor?	Do we want the former owner as an advisor?
Will the buyer run the business as well as I did?	Can we run the business better than the seller did?
Shall I move my home?	Shall we relocate the operation?
What happens if the buyer is unsuccessful?	If this acquisition fails, can we survive?
Shall I buy another business?	Should we build this business up, then sell it?

Buying or selling a well-established, on-going manufacturing business is a traumatic event no matter how smoothly the transaction occurs. It often represents the end of a life's work for the seller and the beginning of a most important event in the life of the buyer. If the buyer is another small corporation or a group of private investors, the results of the transactions could determine the future success or failure of the new owners.

14

The New Owner

You are the buyer and have just completed the closing on the purchase and sale of the Progressive Putty Knife Manufacturing Company. You managed to scrape together the $125,000 down payment and borrow $875,000 in order to present the seller with $1 million in cash. Current sales are at the annual rate of $2 million with estimated earnings after tax of $150,000 per year. The world is your oyster.

This is the end of the party for the seller, who is now a millionaire. It is probably the beginning of the most important responsibility you have ever assumed and it can provide you with satisfaction and enjoyment for years to come.

What do you do now?

If you've been working on this deal for some time, you already know all the key people in the company and you have thought about the future of the enterprise. An important function of the chief executive and principal stockholder of any corporation is to establish the goals for the company and develop plans to achieve these goals. It is now an appropriate time to gather your key people and present your goals and plans.

The circumstances of this meeting should be somewhat formal but comfortable for your employees, perhaps at some location other than the factory: a private dining room in a nice restaurant or a special meeting room in a nearby conference center.

You should give your audience a brief resume of your experience and, if the acquirer is a corporation, the history of the acquiring corporation. Then review the history of the acquired company and point out the logic and advantages of the acquisition. Be sure to mention new opportunities for the key employees and your policy on "participative management" if you subscribe to this type of leadership. Now is the time to win the loyalty and support of your managers and any encouragement that you can give them will pay rich dividends.

To be sure that everyone understands what is expected of them, you should supply each manager with a copy of your written plan that clearly describes the goals which have been established. How the company will achieve these goals is a matter for discussion with your managers. You want them to implement the plan themselves; therefore, you must ask them how they expect to participate, what they believe their job and responsibilities are, and how they can contribute to the success of the organization. You must be prepared to give plenty of advice and guidance and set an example in leadership.

Each manager should provide you with a copy of his or her job description. Study these carefully and see if they describe the responsibilities and duties that are appropriate for the individual as well as the organization. Sooner or later you are going to have to evaluate the performance of your managers and you can't do it effectively if the job description isn't complete and correct (see sample job description in Appendix B).

If your initial appraisal of the management team does not meet your standards or the potential you think is achievable, then you may wish to introduce a management development program to meet the objectives you have established for the company. This program should be tailor-made for those managers with whom you are working. An example of such a program, called "the closed-loop case" method, is shown in Appendix D. This is one of the management training programs that we originated in our company to try to improve management effectiveness. It was successful.

Leadership is a vital element of success in a small company. Large companies can survive with mediocre leadership but small companies quickly succumb to the effects of management incompetence. A small company with 50 years of success can go belly-up within months after changing ownership if the new chief executive officer is not qualified. Qualifications of the owner/manager are discussed in Chapter 3. If you feel that you do not have these qualifications, you should find someone who is qualified or you will find yourself without a company.

If the buyer is another successful small company, it is assumed that you, the buyer, have learned the secrets of success and can bring them to the acquired company. Our experience indicates that success tends to breed success. However, integrating a new acquisition with another company has plenty of pitfalls, the most common of which seems to be the human tendency to resist change. This can be overcome by careful planning and close attention to the human factors of the situation. All people in both the acquired and acquiring companies should be briefed on the merger. Managers should be brought in at an early stage and delegated specific responsibilities and authority.

It is essential that the customers and suppliers of the acquired company be given careful consideration. You may wish to consolidate certain common administrative functions such as purchasing and accounting, and such operational functions as machining, heat treating, and shipping.

This decision may mean early retirement, layoffs, or retraining for some employees of either company. It should also entail opportunities and job enrichment, especially for the middle management of both companies. The best solution to excess employees is to expand sales rapidly so that you need all current employees.

In the final analysis, the merging of two compatible companies or the acquisition of a single company by new owners should produce many good things for the owners, managers, employees, and society in general.

15

The New Millionaire

When you are the seller of a successful small manufacturing business, one of your first duties after the closing will be the happy problem of figuring the taxes you owe on all of the money you have just made.

You hand this job to your accountant as you go to the bank to deposit a sizable check. You have some consolation that you get the benefit of all that cash for at least a few weeks, perhaps a few months.

Don't make any serious plans until you add up and pay all of the expenses of selling your company and collecting all of the receivables. If the deal was a leveraged buyout and you are holding most of the paper, try not to be nervous about the possibility of getting the company back as a basket case.

If you haven't made any retirement plans and don't know where to go after you sell your office, write a book. There are lots of small business owners who would like to know how you managed to get $1 million for your company.

The former owner of a successful manufacturing company should have planned his or her life to disengage gradually from the business and let a well-trained and competent management team take over. But this seldom happens. The business owner who is forced to sell because of lack of success, illness, or poor planning suffers not only the trauma of defeat but the almost certain impoverishment of personal net worth.

In the United States, a business owner who is selling out ought to have unencumbered income-producing assets of at least $1 million that are capable of producing a reliable annual income of $50,000–$75,000 per year. These assets should be capable of appreciating at a rate no less than the average inflation rate.

If the retired business owner ends up with less than this, some academicians might say he or she has not achieved comfortable financial success. Of course there are other ways to measure success and many generous and philanthropic business owners get more satisfaction from giving than receiving. They end their careers in the glory of the elder statesman who helps others to achieve happiness through the work ethic. Not a bad way to go, at all.

Although it is nice to be asked to sit on the board or be an advisor to the new owner, the real romance of the business is gone when you step down as the chief executive or controlling stockholder. But there are growing opportunities for retired small business executives.

The population of the United States will probably be 250 million by 1990. Thus an executive of 65 retiring in 1986 has seen a net population increase in the United States during his or her lifetime of over 100 million. This growth has created a lot of problems and opportunities. To cope with the problems we have become a highly regulated society with an unbelievable infrastructure and rules on how we have to live and conduct our businesses. Today's small business manager alone can no longer assimilate all the information needed to run a business effectively. Retired business owners can help fill this gap by being directors and advisors.

Some of the areas where small businesses need help are the following:

1. Employee rights and responsibilities. There are new and complex regulations on hiring and firing, working conditions, fringe benefits, work place safety, retirement plans, work rules, and smoking rules.

2. Environmental protection. Almost every manufacturing business produces or uses some materials that affect the environment: solvents, cutting fluids, detergents, toxic chemicals, heavy metals, plating or painting materials, dust.

3. Noise. The present acceptable continuous noise level in a factory is 90 decibels.

4. Occupational Safety and Health Administration (OSHA). Machine guards, railings, stairwells, fire doors, stacking limits, walkways, and so on are all specified and regulated.

5. Product liability. Changing laws and public sentiment has brought disaster to many small companies.

6. Electronic Data Processing (EDP). This is virtually unknown in many small manufacturing companies. Where it is being used for the first time, there are horror stories of start-up snafu's, incredible and uncontrollable errors, garbage in and garbage out.

7. Management information systems (MIS). These have not yet trickled down to many smaller companies.

Experienced executives could be very helpful in developing the use of this valuable management tool in small companies.

8. Inventory control. Few small manufacturers have achieved ideal inventory levels or control.

9. Management. Fifty percent of all manufacturing companies with $250,000 to $10 million annual sales are not managed as effectively as they could be if there were fewer top management errors in judgment.

10. Sex and age discrimination. Within the last few years workers have acquired legal rights protecting them from sex or age discrimination. Many small company owners are not up-to-date in this area.

16

Looking Back

Owning and operating your own manufacturing company can be one of the most satisfying careers imaginable for the entrepreneur who craves the ultimate challenge. This is my conclusion after 27 years of such experience. During this time I have met and exchanged ideas with hundreds of other small company owners, managers and would-be entrepreneurs.

In looking back on these happy and rewarding years, I find that there seems to be a recognizable management style among successful entrepreneurs that is worth reviewing. Some of the special characteristics of this style are readily apparent in the previous chapters of this book. Others are not so obvious.

PEOPLE

It is my perception that the most successful small enterprise owner/managers have an unusual ability to motivate their employees; not only their employees but all people with whom they associate: customers, suppliers, lawyers, accountants, bankers, even politicians. I believe that this special talent to motivate comes from the owner/managers' enthusiasm for and dedication to the responsibilities they have chosen to assume. There is no successful entrepreneur who did not wish to be one.

Entrepreneurs expect a lot from others. They have high standards of performance, sometimes too high. This may lead to failure unless they quickly learn to balance achievement with pragmatism.

DECISION MAKING

It has been said that a bad decision can be better than no decision. One characteristic that appears to be typical of the entrepreneur is his or her lack of indecision, or, to put it more positively, his or her decisiveness.

Owner/managers have to make a great deal of decisions daily, everything from how many catalogs to order from the printer today to the size of the marketing budget for next year. Many can make these decisions intuitively with amazing accuracy and good judgment simply based on their ability to absorb and retain a lot of detail. As their business grows and becomes more complex they lose track of some of the details that are properly delegated to others but still they have a strong sense of what's right and what's wrong for the business and can perceive anomalies and aberrations a mile away.

Some entrepreneurs of my acquaintance generally concede that management mistakes are frequent in small manufacturing businesses. One very successful owner of a fast-growing, high-technology company told me that he felt quite comfortable if 51% of his decisions turned out well. To be wrong or ineffective 49% of the time may seem like operating on the very edge of disaster, however, if you look at your record objectively you might shrug your shoulders and say, "Well, maybe that's right."

If you can accept the idea of your own fallibility you might be willing to speed up your decision making, feel better about taking risks, and not get too upset about being wrong or ineffective occasionally. After all, entrepreneurism is the freedom to make mistakes and the wisdom to correct them.

CRITICAL CHOICES

Failure of entrepreneurs generally takes place at a time of critical choices. These often involve strategic decisions that have to be based on an estimate of the situation that, in turn, is dependent on essential elements of information. A lack of reliable information can flaw your estimate of the situation. As a result you could prescribe a disastrous or ineffective strategy. This is the kind of error that is hard to detect and difficult to correct.

To be adequately prepared to make critical choices you must constantly assimilate information about conditions in your industry. You must be informed on your existing and potential markets; you must be up-to-date on the state of the art in your manufacturing; you should be in regular touch with key customers, key suppliers, and trade associations; and you must keep close track of your competition. The emphasis of your leadership activity should be on:

Anticipation rather than reaction

Opportunities rather than problems

The future rather than the past

The marketplace rather than the factory

Planned rather than random activity

Results rather than style

TRAINING

In our constant search for excellence, we discovered that our most valuable resource was our employees. However, incompletely trained employees are an undeveloped resource. The entrepreneur must find ways to develop and use all the individual and collective talents available right in his or her own factory. Many entrepreneurs consider on-the-job training (often by fellow workers) to be adequate in a small business but merely showing an employee what to do and how to do it is not enough. It is important to show your managers and workers how they fit into the overall plans and policies of the enterprise and how they can contribute to its success, hence to their own success.

There are many ways to train and motivate people. We developed a method of training our managers which we call the "closed-loop" case method (see Appendix D) in which actual management problems and opportunities were presented to the managers in a classroom style. Solutions to the cases were sought through a team effort which developed management analysis and decision-making skills. We feel that we have enriched careers and made a good management better.

Although the measurement and control of human error is a very imprecise art it should be high on the list of important functions of the entrepreneur.

MARKETING

One of the most common causes of small business failure is poor marketing skills. The U.S. Patent Office is overflowing with new product ideas that never got to market. And for every patented product that failed to sell there are probably 100 nonpatented products that never saw the marketplace. Of course, many were not practical or were never intended to be sold. However, the good ideas that died aborning might have been successful if they had had the benefit of a good marketing effort.

Marketing is not only the selling of a product or service, it includes all of the activities necessary to try to be competitively successful in the marketplace:

Market research and analysis

Advertising and sales promotion

Publicity

Distribution analysis

Competition analysis

Foreign sales potential

Sales training

Customer relations

Product news bulletins

Whether you are a buyer or a seller of a small manufacturing company you must see that your marketing function is first class. For the buyer, a good product with a poor sales history can indicate an opportunity to apply better marketing techniques. It can also signal a saturated market or a product that is growing obsolete.

A good marketing team can not only secure orders and increase your sales but can spot flaws and opportunities in the marketing functions of acquisition prospects. They are trained to do this. So when you are buying or selling look closely and critically at the sales history.

PLANNING

As mentioned previously, random activity toward indefinite goals leads nowhere. Many small companies are run in this manner. The astute buyer will quickly recognize the aimlessness of the target company and may find a golden opportunity for his or her organizing and planning abilities.

I have emphasized the importance of planning in Chapters 4 and 5. Those who do not plan well will not fare well. They are constant victims of unanticipated events and their expectations are a mere wish list. Planning requires articulation, the ability to think precisely and express ideas interestingly and above all, clearly. In our company we have five sectors of planning:

1. *Strategic Plan.* This is the responsibility of top management. It attempts to predict where we will be in five years and how we are going to get there. A strategic plan is always subject to changes and adjustments but it gives the enterprise a strong sense of purpose and direction. A good plan forces you into creativity, research, exploration, and critical analysis. Properly done strategic planning will enrich the careers of your top management team.

2. *Tactical Plan.* The strategic plan should call for one year tactical plans which answer the question, "What are we going to do in the next 12 months?" In many companies this is called the budget and all categories of income and expense are forecast for the year. These figures are provided by departmental or divisional managers the principal ones of which are marketing, manufacturing, and financial.

The budget is prepared in such a way that monthly or quarterly actual performance figures can be posted and compared to forecast. This is often the principal subject of conversation at quarterly board meetings and monthly or weekly staff meetings. If you constantly exceed or fall short of budget, you better go back to the plan to see if enough effort has gone into it to make it worthwhile. Incidentally, performance against budget is often used as a measure of management effectiveness.

3. *Marketing Plan.* The largest and most detailed plan we have in our company is the annual marketing plan. In this plan we forecast the sales of every product line, the amount of every category of marketing expense from postage to salaries, and a detailed advertising plan. The total sales volume of all products and services is the sales revenue in the budget. This is the most important of all annual plans in our company. Although we are a manufacturing enterprise with all of the usual challenges of running a factory and making

a high-quality product, we consider the marketing of our products to be our strongest advantage.

4. *Manufacturing Plan.* The vice president of manufacturing is required to submit an annual plan showing what is needed to fulfill the sales forecast. This includes inventory projections, capital equipment requirements, personnel and housekeeping (security, janitorial services, building and grounds maintenance, etc.).

The most difficult decision for the manufacturing management is to decide how accurate the sales forecast is.

5. *Financial Plan.* The controller, treasurer, or vice president of finance is responsible for the financial plan for the year and also the compilation of the company budget. A pro forma profit and loss statement and a balance sheet are prepared. These management documents are used as a basis to measure the progress of the company over the ensuing 12 months. They are not sacred and should be changed if circumstances require it.

Cash flow for the year should be carefully and conservatively estimated so that there is no slow down in paying bills or other obligations. If additional working capital is needed a line of credit should already be in place and borrowing requires only a routine call to the bank.

CREATIVITY

Most of the successful small companies that I know are blessed with creative leadership and innovative management. This seems to be the main source of fun for the entrepreneur: thinking up new ideas, products, services, and ways in which the enterprise can grow.

But creativity need not be or seldom is limited to products

and services. It can be applied to the way in which the company is run, how it treats its employees, what it does for the community, and what influence the company exerts in its industry.

The Small Business Association of New England (SBANE) is a typical organization for and led by small business owner/managers. Having been a member of this association for many years we had the opportunity to meet hundreds of other entrepreneurs most of whom displayed remarkable creativeness. Although the membership is augmented by plenty of non-New Englanders, they all take great pride in their "Yankee Ingenuity." Creativity in business can be learned. The SBANE folks are a good example.

RESULTS

The buzzword "bottom line" refuses to fade from the small business lexicon therefore I would like to use it to describe the results that owner/managers overuse frequently to refer to their net earnings. The real estate industry has embellished this term with "triple-net" bottom line (meaning net after tax, interest and all other expense). What everyone is talking about is the final result of operating or investing in a for-profit enterprise.

Colorful style and innovative methodology are characteristic of many small companies but they do not necessarily contribute to the bottom line. The essential element of successful results is good leadership. In the final analysis the results are what count and this is what you are looking for as a buyer or a seller of a small manufacturing business. *Cave Canem!*

Acquisition Proposal, Marsh Manufacturing Company, Portland, Oregon

HISTORY

The Marsh Manufacturing Company was founded in 1917 by Gordon Marsh and David Taylor for the purpose of manufacturing logging tools and machinery for the lumbering industry.

In the early days Marsh made cant hooks, peevees, lance poles, boat hooks, ladders, and other products of wood and metal mostly for the forest and marine industries but also specialized in ladders for fire trucks.

World War I hero General John Albright Tucker was associated with the business in its early days as an owner and member of the board of directors.

The company was highly regarded by the Portland business community according to numerous newspaper and trade paper clippings found in the company's historical files and revealed by former and retired employees still living in the Portland area. At one time there were over 200 employees on the payroll.

CORPORATE STRUCTURE

The company started as a partnership of Marsh and Taylor in 1917 and was incorporated on March 17, 1922, shortly after the death of David Taylor whose share was sold to Gordon Marsh. There are presently 100,000 shares authorized with 94,231 shares issued and outstanding.

OFFICERS AND DIRECTORS

Five officers are active in the business, as follows:

President: Ellsworth Marsh, 63, son of Gordon Marsh, 27 years with company and largest stockholder. Graduate of Amherst College and the Harvard Business School. Division manager and vice president of Clarke and Davis in Eureka, California (a large lumber company) prior to employment with Marsh.

Vice President–Marketing: George Fossel, 54, 18 years with company. Graduate of Stanford University.

Vice President–Manufacturing: Henry Lockwood, 47, 12 years with company. Engineering degree from University of Oregon. Previously with Ampex as manager of manufacturing engineering.

Vice President–Finance: Thomas Lombardi, 54, eight years with company. Degree in finance and CPA, University of California, Los Angeles. Formerly with Peat, Marwick and Mitchell in Portland.

Secretary–Treasurer: Charles Marsh, 32, son of Ellsworth Marsh. BA degree from Amherst College, MBA from Stanford University. Five years with Lockheed as administrative assistant to vice president of finance.

The seven directors include Ellsworth Marsh, Charles Marsh, George Fossel, Henry Lockwood, and three outside directors:

Alexander Worthington: President, CEO, and principal stockholder of the Ames Manufacturing Company, makers of industrial machinery.

Benjamin R. Proctor: Vice president for research and development with Lockheed Aircraft Corporation.

Alice M. Hutchins: Vice president of the Portland National Bank where Marsh Manufacturing is an important and valued client.

STOCK OWNERSHIP

The 94,231 shares of stock outstanding are closely held in the Marsh family and the family maintains active control of the company. There are about 15 stockholders (all members of the family). Ellsworth Marsh and Charles Marsh together own 50,000 shares.

ORGANIZATION

The management control is organized along very conventional lines with clear and specific job descriptions for every job in the company. These job descriptions are used for defining responsibilities and evaluating performance. The organization chart is as follows:

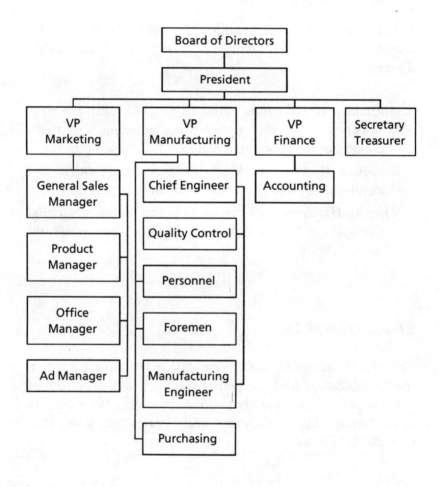

MANAGEMENT PHILOSOPHY

General

All employees are aware that management considers the company's employees to be its most valuable resource. Special training programs are conducted by the company continuously to up-grade employee performance and productivity. Management claims that their training programs are responsible for the consistently above average earnings of the company.

Growth

The company has shown a steady growth in sales and earnings every year except two since its inception. Growth has been achieved through new products, very creative marketing techniques (many of which originated in Marsh Manufacturing), and the acquisition of other companies. In April 1986 Marsh received information indicating that Harold Hardware (a competitor) was for sale. Contact was made with the management and negotiations are under way for Marsh to purchase this company. Details are available to serious prospects.

Management insists on detailed annual planning and forecasting as well as strategic (five-year) planning.

Public Image

The management makes a special effort to participate in affairs that present an opportunity to develop a favorable public image. They are active in local and national special interest groups (civic matters, education, environment, etc.) and in trade and professional associations.

Special Factors

The present management of the company has achieved a high degree of leadership quality that may not be sustainable under new or different management. They claim that this is a "learnable" skill and cannot only be maintained but can be transferred to other operations and can be further refined and improved. This concept should be accepted with caution and reservations.

LEGAL

The company has no serious legal problems at present. They have had several product liability suits (none in the past three years) and all were settled for nominal payments. Corporate counsel is Mather, Jones, Edgeworth and Nelson. Legal costs average about $4000 per year.

ACCOUNTING

The current accountant is Peat, Marwick and Mitchell. There are no special accounting requirements and accounting fees have averaged about $18,000 per year ($39,500 in 1983 when the Holson Machine Company was acquired).

FINANCIAL

Dividends have been paid irregularly depending on the financial needs (or perceived needs) of the company. Last year a $2.50 per share dividend was paid. In 1980, $5.00 was paid. The company has been overly concerned about the "unreasonable accumulation of profits." Their growth and acquisition plans are more than adequate to justify retention of all earnings.

BORROWING

The company frequently has no long-term debt and the balance sheet is consistently very conservative with cash and marketable securities often exceeding total liabilities.

PROFIT AND LOSS STATEMENTS

Here is a 10-year summary of sales and earnings including per share figures.

	Sales (000)	After-Tax Earnings (000)	Per Share	Earnings as % of Sales
1985	20,407	1,703	18.07	8.34%
1984	18,683	1,382	14.66	7.39
1983	18,001	1,294	13.73	7.18
1982	17,770	1,315	13.95	7.40

	Sales (000)	After-Tax Earnings (000)	Per Share	Earnings as % of Sales
1981	16,509	1,192	12.65	7.22
1980	14,753	894	9.48	6.05
1979	14,876	1,003	10.64	6.74
1978	12,133	994	10.55	8.19
1977	10,852	872	9.25	8.03
1976	9,106	709	7.52	7.78
Forecast for 1986–1987				
1986	22,115	1,800		8.14
1987	25,000	2,250		9.00

Copies of audited financial statements for the last five years are available.

BUDGETS

Preliminary budgets for one year in advance are carefully prepared each year by November 1 and finalized in January for the then-current year. These are used as a control on both sales and expense. Management gives the budget considerable weight in making decisions. If sales goals are not met and there are no extenuating circumstances, management insists on expense adjustments even if an important capital expense has to be postponed. The current budget versus actual is attached.

REPORTS

Monthly reports are required for sales and estimated earnings. Figures to date are presented and discussed in monthly management meetings, and compared to budget. Significant deviations are always noted and corrective action discussed if appropriate.

INVENTORY

Management tries to keep inventory turning over at about three to four times per year. However, this is not well controlled and represents an area of weakness in management that could be improved.

Management claims that astute buying (at bargain prices) and excellent customer service justify the occasional overage in inventory. This may be true but the improvement in earnings in the last three years with a fairly stable inventory (not over $5 million at any time) indicates that they have carried too much inventory in the past.

FIXED ASSETS

Fixed assets cost $6,257,813 with depreciation of $2,364,504, or a net book value of $3,893,309. A recent appraisal put a fair market value on these assets of more than $8 million.

MARKETING

General

Marsh Manufacturing has a very superior and innovative marketing department to which much of its success can be attributed. It sells through more than 3000 distributors, dealers, and agents with nearly 10% of its sales to foreign countries. It also has over $5 million in annual sales to OEM and private brand customers and nearly $1 million in direct retail sales to customers not served through normal distribution channels.

SALES PERSONNEL

In addition to the headquarters staff of four product managers and eight inside sales personnel, there are four regional field sales managers at warehouse locations in Los Angeles, Chicago, New York, and Portland who are responsible for local distribution and sales to all major accounts in their areas.

ADVERTISING

Personal selling, trade paper advertising, and direct mail are the principal means of promoting the company's products. Trade shows and special exhibits are also done on a regular basis. The advertising and sales promotion budget has been established by management at about 3% of sales. This is somewhat less than the average for the industry but Marsh's advertising efficiency is unquestionably superior to its competitors.

COMPETITION

Marsh Manufacturing Company is recognized as the leader in its field. Most competitors follow Marsh's pricing practices. The five principal competitive manufacturers (with estimated annual sales) are:

Union Manufacturing, Augusta, Maine—20,000,000

Acme Ladder Company, Des Moines, Iowa—18,000,000

Pettigrew & Davis, Ashville, North Carolina—12,000,000

Jasper P. Withington & Sons, Putnam, Connecticut—8,000,000

Harold Hardware, Memphis, Tennessee—5,000,000

MANUFACTURING

Marsh was a pioneer in developing special manufacturing techniques in its industry. Engineers there designed and built special machinery, some of which is so unique that no outsider is allowed a look. No prospective buyer can see the machinery until a sales agreement is executed.

Marsh has always claimed that it was the leader in the manufacturing technology in this industry, and strong evidence supports the claim. Henry Lockwood, vice president of manufacturing, is well known and highly respected in the industry. The president of the woodworking guild, George R. MacDonald, was quoted in the October 17, 1982 *Oregon Post* as saying that Henry Lockwood has more patents issued to him for woodworking tools and machinery than any other person in the United States.

Of the total employment of 183 employees in June 1985, 120 were directly or indirectly involved in manufacturing. The company does not now have and never has had a union. In 1933 there was an attempt by the Longshore Union to organize Marsh but it was voted down by a large margin. Many second- and third-generation families work at Marsh and, in interviews conducted on May 15, 1985, expressed a strong loyalty to the company and satisfaction in employee relations.

FACILITIES

Marsh occupies one large, modern single-story building on 23 acres of prime industrial land on Columbia Boulevard south of the City of Portland, Oregon. The size of the building is 95,000 square feet and is owned by the Marsh Real Estate Company. The rent is shown in the profit and loss statement at $475,000 per year ($5.00 per square foot) and has been at this rate for three years.

The current rent is low for this type of facility and will probably be raised to $6.00 per square foot within the next 18 months. However, the building and land are being offered for sale at $3,600,000.

Public water and sewer are included and there is adequate and inexpensive electric power now in place.

The real estate company also owns two of its four warehouses (in Los Angeles and Chicago), on which Marsh pays very reasonable rent ($3.00 per square foot in Chicago and $4.00 in Los Angeles) and has an option to purchase the New York warehouse. The owned warehouses and option on the New York building are for sale for $700,000. These are all first-class buildings in excellent locations with attractive office space and will undoubtedly increase in value. In the New York building there is extra space that is now subleased.

COMMENTARY

The Marsh Manufacturing Company is an unusually well managed company that is offered at a premium price of approximately $10 million. If profit margins can be maintained or improved, the price is not excessive. However, there is considerable risk in losing the innovative leadership of Ellsworth Marsh, who will not continue as CEO but would agree to serve on the board of the acquiring company for $50,000 per year for five years (part of this could be a noncompete agreement).

George Fossel, vice president of marketing of Marsh, is a dynamic and talented executive and would be the logical successor to Mr. Marsh. He has agreed to accept the position of CEO with a five-year contract. The chief executive of Harold Hardware, with whom Marsh is now negotiating, is Gilbert Chatsworth. He is also a possibility as CEO of Marsh and seems to be well qualified. No discussions have been had with Chatsworth. He would be available only if Marsh is successful in acquiring Harold Hardware and only if a thorough investigation reveals that he has all of the qualities required.

Sample Job Description Position Title: President Supervision: Board of Directors

The basic functions of this position are to establish corporate objectives with the help and approval of the board of directors and the stockholders, to develop ideas and plans to achieve these objectives, to supervise, guide, and counsel subordinates in the accomplishment of their responsibilities (as described in their job descriptions), to identify and control all resources required for the success of the company, and to provide wise and practical leadership to the enterprise.

AREAS OF MAJOR RESPONSIBILITY

Major responsibility areas are:

1. Resource management
2. Performance standards
3. External affairs
4. Reports and proposals
5. Special projects

Resource Management

Responsibilities

Determine resources required, the level of quality desired, and the source.

Key Duties

Supervise and participate in the search, hiring, and training of key management personnel.
   Study and plan for the financial needs of the company.
   Supervise the development of:

Productive resources
New products
New markets
New activities

Study the need and recommend the use of outside help where we do not have in-house capabilities.
   Supervise the acquisition of other assets.

Performance Standards

Responsibilities

Establish standards of performance in the management of the company and develop ways to achieve excellence.

Key Duties

Prepare job descriptions with performance criteria.
Evaluate performance.
Study and recommend incentive programs.
Establish training programs.
Weed out substandard performance.

External Affairs

Responsibilities

Identify, evaluate, and monitor external influences and special interests that may affect the company and recommend appropriate action.

Key Duties

Keep well-informed on business and economic events and determine their impact on company plans and operations.

Circulate and participate in outside educational and business activities that will provide intelligence, experience, and opportunities useful to the company. Serve on other suitable boards with approval of stockholders.

Support trade associations, special interest groups, and activities that can be helpful to the company.

Reports and Proposals

Responsibilities

Establish a steady flow of reports and intelligence that can be used to evaluate the performance of the company and to guide the management and stockholders in making plans and decisions.

Key Duties

Supervise the preparation of certified annual financial statements.

Prepare interpretations of financial statements.

Submit monthly sales and cash reports.

Prepare budgets and cash flow projections.

Submit annual reports on all separately identifiable operations.

Submit annual review and update on goals and objectives.

Prepare fair market value estimates on all assets.

Review all internal reports.

Special Projects

Responsibilities

Identify, define, and recommend action on important but unanticipated problems and opportunities. These are frequently of critical importance to the company and management action must be prompt and appropriate.

Key Duties

Be alert constantly for the first signs of problems. Act quickly and positively to prevent them from spreading. Don't leave them until they are solved.

Develop problem recognition and solving skills among subordinates.

Learn to turn problems into opportunities.

Constantly search for new opportunities to improve operations, to improve skills and techniques, to acquire other assets, to make the enterprise superior in every respect.

QUALIFICATIONS DESIRED

1. College graduate, preferably with advanced degree in business management
2. Strong leadership ability
3. Unusual creative ability
4. Market oriented
5. At least 10 years of progressively increasing responsibility in marketing and/or general management

METHODS OF MEASURING PERFORMANCE

1. Attainment of sales and earnings goals in manufacturing divisions.
2. Attainment of objectives for nonmanufacturing investments especially in appreciation.
3. Opinions and comments of employees, customers, suppliers, and business associates.
4. Accomplishments outside the job responsibility: directorships, community activities, publications, activities in trade associations.

5. Ideas originated and successfully executed.

6. Project performance.

POSITIONS FOR WHICH THIS PERSON SHOULD BE FULLY QUALIFIED AFTER 10 YEARS OF EXPERIENCE AND SUPERIOR PERFORMANCE

1. President of another medium-sized manufacturing company

2. Vice president of large corporation

3. Director of other similar-sized companies

4. Trustee of private educational institution

5. Undersecretary of Commerce, U.S. Department of Commerce

6. President of industrial trade association

Outline of Actual Seller's Business Plan

This is the outline of the actual plan of a communications company in a loss situation looking for a buyer:

A. Nature and description of business
   1. Company
   2. Industry
B. History of company
   1. Founder
   2. Growth pattern
   3. Strengths and weaknesses
C. Technology
   1. Background
   2. Present "state of the art"
   3. Future of the industry

D. Market analysis
   1. History of sales
   2. Market share
   3. Future trends
   4. Copies of all literature and advertising
E. Strategic planning
   1. Assumptions
   2. Opportunities
   3. Objectives (5 million in sales in five years)
   4. Plan to achieve objectives
   5. Financial projections
F. Management
   1. Organization chart
   2. Job description
   3. Resumés of managers
   4. Team accomplishments
G. Financial analysis
   1. Financial statements—five years actual
   2. Performance against budget
   3. Projections
H. Valuations
   1. Fixed assets
   2. Inventory
   3. Real estate
   4. Goodwill
   5. Copies of appraisals

The Closed-Loop Case*

How can smaller companies get their managers and supervisors to focus on operational problems and business opportunities in a nonthreatening and interesting way? One means is by using a modified version of the case method, which many business schools have employed successfully. Because the cases start and end within the company, the author calls the approach the "closed-loop" case method. Top managers ask other officials for suggestions about company situations needing attention. Then the top executives pick out the most frequently mentioned areas and gather information necessary to write cases. Assembled in small groups, managers discuss the cases and ways for resolving them — all the time avoiding placing blame and seeking scapegoats.

The author says that once the cases' nonthreatening nature becomes clear, participants often become quite involved in the discussions. More important, he argues, the solutions generated by case discussions can improve operations and profits.

Because small companies usually can't afford to hire all the managerial talent they need, they simply do without. Unknown to their owners, many of these companies have a pool of excellent management talent: their employees. With proper training, these employees could relieve top executives of many managerial tasks and at the same time improve overall productivity.

My company has found the case method of teaching to be an excellent way to prepare employees for management tasks. Our use of the case method stems from our practice, begun in 1960, of sending a few managers and potential managers to small business seminars at business schools. Ever since then, the company's long-range management effectiveness has improved.

A few years ago, the company decided to use a case method of problem and opportunity analysis, similar to that taught in these schools, to solve in-house problems. After much debate and reflection, we developed the idea into a formal training program. We made clear from the start that the purpose of the program was not to find fault or place blame but to improve individual and group performance in recognizing opportunities and finding solutions to problems. More specifically, our goals were to:

Help managers be more productive

Recognize more opportunities

Solve more problems

Develop a strong sense of helpful involvement

We called our approach the closed-loop case method because the cases started and ended within our company.

If properly planned and executed, this training method has several advantages for the small company:

New insights into company problems

Immediate and continuous access to all the facts in the case

Development of solutions that can be put into practice

Continuous feedback on the progress of the solutions

Fine-tuning of the management team's skills while giving its members a real sense of productive participation

Moving the case method from the college classroom to the factory proved to be more difficult than we expected. Although some of our managers had MBAs and others had been exposed to case studies in seminars, nearly half of our student–managers had no previous experience with the case method. Therefore, we held several orientation meetings to explain our intentions and expectations. We had participants answer a simple questionnaire that was designed to identify our priority management training areas (see Exhibit I).

At first, some managers were reluctant to point us toward problems in which they were personally involved. They were also hesitant to identify problems they perceived to be outside their specialties. We realized that managers closely associated with particular problems or opportunities might become hostile if we questioned their action or lack of action. We tried to mitigate their understandable reaction by getting everyone to reaffirm that hindsight is better than foresight and that a timely but risky positive action is more desirable than no action at all. Happily, after the first few cases, which did not involve personalities, participants decided that we weren't looking for scapegoats but for solutions and opportunities.

THE PROGRAM'S MECHANICS

The program is organized so that two groups of eight or nine managers meet in two-hour sessions once a month. We wanted to accommodate work schedules and allow the participants to switch from one group to the other when necessary. We assign participating managers to the groups so that all leadership functions are evenly represented. A typical distribution is shown in the insert [closed-loop participants]. As it turned out, the first two groups developed divergent perspectives on several of the cases, which added a valuable dimension to their discussions.

CLOSED-LOOP PARTICIPANTS

Group A	Group B
President (moderator)	Moderator[*]
Vice president, marketing	Vice president, manufacturing
Chief engineer	Sales manager
Advertising manager	Office manager
Foreman, Division A	Foreman, Division B
Purchasing agent	Controller
Accounting manager	Administrative assistant
Foreman, Division C	General foreman
Traffic manager	Product manager

[*] We hired an independent professional training consultant especially for this assignment.

Based on the participants' questionnaire responses and their informal suggestions for case subjects, we formulate the cases from a list of all company problems, projects, and opportunities that seem suitable. At the outset, we received over 50 acceptable suggestions and chose 10 cases to start the program:

1. Assignment of spaces in the parking lots
2. The repair department
3. Production control
4. New product development
5. Performance evaluation
6. Market research
7. Underestimated success
8. Customer service
9. The computer
10. The night shift

These topics represented a range of problems: those that had never been adequately addressed, those that were just emerging, and those that we would inevitably face in the future. We also wanted to single out areas of opportunity for the company, such as improving resource management.

Participants' job titles indicate their obvious lack of knowledge or experience in some of the case areas. This is intentional. We want all of our managers to participate in problem and opportunity analysis outside their specialties. We expect this experience to at once broaden their involvement in company affairs and uncover hidden strengths and interests that can benefit the company. In this way, we have identified talents among our managers that are useful in solving other problems.

WRITING THE CASES

Presenting closed-loop cases is a challenge quite different from presenting academic cases. In an academic case, students have no information other than the material written and edited by the case writer. Nor do they have access to the subject company or the case writer.

In our closed-loop cases, we not only provide on paper what we believe to be the essential facts, but we also encourage our participants to do research in our factory if they want additional information. We take care, however, not to create disruption or conflict in the workplace.

Our standard procedure for preparing cases is to provide some background on the problem or opportunity. It is very important to avoid issues of personality. Our feeling is that errors, omissions, and ineffective actions are the ultimate responsibility of the company's leadership, which we are trying to improve in this training program.

A typical case is shown in Exhibit II. It identifies and describes the problem area. You will note that some information is indefinite or subjective. Because we find that our problem analysis tends to start in a general fashion with estimates, opinions, and assumptions, we include these in our cases.

ADJUSTING TO THE PROCESS

The participants receive the cases two to four weeks before each monthly meeting, which allows them time for reading and research. Each participant is expected to ask questions and to offer opinions and suggestions during the classroom discussions.

The classroom discussions usually begin with introductory remarks by one of the company's officers. Once discussion starts, the officer chooses someone at random to lead it. Originally, we had expected to give every class member a chance to lead the discussions, but because some were uncomfortable in this role, we did not pressure anyone to do so. We decided that these people could learn by observing and might become more comfortable leading a discussion once they were better aware of the leadership qualities we were trying to develop. Indeed, by the end of the first phase of the program, many of the students showed a noticeable increase in self-confidence and expressed a willingness (in some cases even an eagerness) to participate.

A moderator controls each meeting to keep the discussion on course and occasionally points out a lesson to be learned. The ideal moderator should have a firsthand knowledge of the business, be familiar to the participants, hold a position of responsibility and respect, and have an aptitude for leadership training. A secretary keeps notes that are later transcribed and delivered to the manager responsible for formulating a plan of action.

The meetings are scheduled to last two hours but often run longer. They resemble business school classes with one important difference—any questions that arise concerning the facts of the case can be easily answered. In several instances, we have called in workers to help us with omitted or disputed facts. Occasionally, participants discover incorrect or misleading information in a case and quickly correct it. Every member of the training group thus learns the importance of accurately and reliably communicating information.

THE BENEFITS AND COSTS

The training group does not produce a plan of action to solve the problem. Rather, it discusses problems, makes suggestions, and often introduces some new and useful ideas.

The manager responsible for the area under discussion must formulate the final plan for resolving the problem. That individual is always present in one of the groups, listening to and participating in the problem analysis. Afterward he or she receives a transcript or summary of both groups' discussions (see Exhibit III).

The manager then prepares and executes an action plan. To determine if the situation has improved, top management reviews the results three to six months later.

So far, we've compiled and discussed ten cases. With six of these cases, including the one described in Exhibit II, we've made real improvements in the company's approach to problem solving. In two cases, we've been unsuccessful, mainly because the case discussions brought out festering personal frictions; indeed, we lost two managers, probably in part because of the discomfort the cases created. Finally, with the last two cases, we came to indifferent conclusions, perhaps because the participants just couldn't become very excited about the issues. One of these cases concerned problems in the parking lot.

When properly presented, closed-loop case histories not only help to identify and develop latent management talent, but they also help resolve problems that small business management might otherwise have to overlook.

The cost of this training in time has been high: probably 50 hours of management time per month. But a remarkable thing has happened. Company sales have increased by more than 10% with very little rise in overhead costs. Inventory has gone down with negligible effect on deliveries.

We can't prove that a significant correlation exists between our training program and improved operations, of
course, but we do like to think it exists.

EXHIBIT I
Blackstone's Employee Questionnaire

This is the form we use to find out our employee's areas of interest.

The purpose of this form is to discover your concerns as managers. Your
replies will point us toward problems or opportunities that we can
develop into case studies. You need not restrict your answers to areas
in which you are personally involved. If you are familiar with problems
or opportunities outside your department, we will certainly consider
them as case studies. Potential topics include company work rules,
fringe benefits, acquisitions, and new products.

Which of these areas interests you?

Operations

These are the repetitive, mechanical tasks we do every day. Operations
functions include information processing (order entry, correspondence,
memos), communications with customers and suppliers, internal communications, production scheduling, and organization.

Control

Involves keeping things going smoothly or preventing things from going
wrong. Controllers plan, organize, set up systems, measure, estimate,
interpret figures, take corrective action, and lead and guide people.

Personnel

Involves judging people's abilities and capacities and getting them into
the right jobs. Personnel managers assign work, train new staff, settle
disputes and conflicts, and try to keep people happy and productive in
their work. Examples of personnel issues include performance reviews,
discipline and grievance procedures, dress codes, and sex and age
discrimination.

Creativity

Involves finding new and better ways to do things. For example, try
studying all the forms you use. Could they be better? Could they be
combined, eliminated, printed on two sides, printed in color, printed
on colored paper, put in pads, taken out of pads, self-mailing, self-
sealing, more attractive? Design something.

Goal Setting

How do I set goals? How do I know that they are appropriate, reasonable, and achievable? In order to set goals, you must identify a problem or opportunity, decide what expectations are reasonable based on your knowledge and experience, define your goal, develop plans, execute them, and measure the results. Goal setting is one of a manager's most difficult jobs.

Problem Identification and Analysis

When goals are not being met and people are indifferent, bored, or unco-operative, how can you determine what's wrong? You've got to define the problem. If you can't define or describe it, you can't resolve it. That's why we want you to give us a case history. It will help you to learn how to identify problems. By analyzing cases, we help each other.

Once a problem is defined it is half-solved. Analyzing the problem means looking at its description, thinking of possible solutions, choosing one that seems appropriate, and then trying it. If it doesn't work, try something else.

Opportunity Recognition

Half of a manager's time should be spent seeking opportunities to do things better, quicker, easier, or cheaper. To improve management effectiveness, we must get our managers to be constantly alert for new ideas.

Judgment

Good judgment cannot be taught. It comes only through knowledge and experience. Our case studies will broaden your knowledge; you can apply what you have learned to your own work. Developing judgment requires that you make clear decisions about what is right and wrong for the company.

Now that you have selected one or more areas of interest, you should try to identify problems or opportunities within those areas. Be prepared to present your choice so that it can be written as a case.

If you do not feel ready to suggest a case study based on your own experience, please indicate some managerial areas that you would like others to pursue as case studies, such as sales or manufacturing.

EXHIBIT II
Case Study

What Can We Do about the Repair Business of Division A?

Division A of Blackstone Industries is a manufacturer of miniature power tools. It was founded in 1922 in New York City with a slogan (still used) of "Quality and Service Since 1922." For 36 years it enjoyed slow, but steady growth under the founders' guidance and reached sales of $300,000 per year. In 1958, Division A was sold to Blackstone Industries and the business flourished, by 1984 achieving annual sales of more than $5 million.

Although Division A has been considered a successful acquisition, several of its operational areas need improvement. One such area is the management of the repair and service department. That is the subject of this case.

The repair department's operation has not changed much in 25 years. It has been run by the same foreman and has followed the same procedures. It functions adequately but it doesn't make money. And customers are not overjoyed with repair service that takes 30 to 45 days. Complaints about repair pricing, however, are few. Here's how a typical repair is handled:

1. The packages are received and opened daily in the receiving department. The receiving department writes the date of receipt on the outside of the box with a large black marker. Within a few hours of receipt, receiving employees load all opened boxes onto a cart that goes to the repair department.

2. The repair department unloads the cart, recording each arrival carefully on a desk calendar. Customer name, date of receipt by the repair department, and a one-word description of the item are entered. After the boxes are all identified and recorded, they are shelved in order of date received.

3. Most repairs have a shipping ticket, order, letter, or note in the box with requests or instructions. These notes are read when the box is first opened in the repair department. The box may then sit on the shelf for 30 days before anyone looks at it. The average time on the shelf is 15 days.

4. The receipt of repairs is not acknowledged to the customer. If customers call or write, workers have to search the calendar and/or the shelf to check the status of the repair. Sometimes, if necessary, the item will be taken off the shelf out of turn.

5. When the repair finally gets to the workbench, the repair person must first determine what's wrong. This usually doesn't take long.

The repair person then has to determine if the cost of repair exceeds 50% of the cost of a new product. If it does, the repair person completes a repair order form and sends it to the sales department, which informs the customer by letter that the cost of repair is more than half of the cost of a new product. Although we now have an opportunity to make a sale, we do not offer the customer any special incentive to buy a new item.

6. If the customer has asked for a quotation on a repair, we send one regardless of the percentage of the cost of a new item the repair cost represents. This procedure tends to delay the repair since the customer would automatically receive the repaired item if the repair cost is less than 50% of the value of a new item.

That is the procedure for handling repairs. Here are some cost and labor factors:

1. Normally we employ an average of $1\frac{1}{2}$ repair persons. The direct labor cost, including fringes, is about $12 an hour.

2. We charge $15 an hour to the customer for repair labor. We charge $8.75 for the first half-hour.

3. The load in the repair department varies by season. Because people tend to send things in for repair when their plants are shut down for inventory or when they go away for a winter vacation, the end of the year is the busiest time. At this time, we lend the repair department part-time helpers. Over a year this extra help might be equivalent to two full-time repair persons. We use that estimate to calculate direct labor repair costs.

4. Indirect costs for the repair department include occupancy, depreciation on machines, supplies, and spare-parts inventory. The last is a large item: We usually spend $20,000 a year for inventory; motor armatures alone cost $5000.

5. If we estimate that a typical monthly repair revenue is about $2000, with labor and benefit costs of $2400, material costs of $500, and indirect costs of $1000, the loss on repair business is $3900–$2000, or $1900 a month.

All manufacturers of durable goods have to live with a repair and service division. It is generally viewed as a nuisance. Yet customers' goodwill depends on the quality and cost of service.

This case is presented to you to stimulate and test your ability to think creatively.

How can you turn this problem into an opportunity?

How can you turn this loss into a profit?

EXHIBIT III
Case Summary

Memorandum

TO: Vice president, marketing

FROM: President

DATE: March 8, 1984

SUBJECT: Repair department case study

FILE: Blackstone management training

On February 15 and 25, groups A and B discussed the Division A repair department case.

The purpose of the case was to determine whether repair operations were being well managed to identify any problems or opportunities that needed attention.

Many thoughtful suggestions were made during the discussions:

1. Increase the labor charge to $25 or $30 an hour.
2. Charge for estimates and credit the charge to customers if they authorize us to make the repair.
3. Collect all statistical copies of repair orders and review them periodically.
4. Charge 10% for restocking and handling if an item is returned for credit and the fault is not ours.
5. Offer the customer a trade-in allowance on a new item if the cost of repair is greater than half the price of a new unit. The allowance would have to be different for dealer and retail accounts but it should be easy to work out a schedule.
6. Acknowledge receipt of the customer's repair promptly.
7. The 70 to 100 customers who send repairs each month should be treated as old friends and new prospects. Do something nice for them. Send them our latest catalogs. Develop a folksy letter. Ask them to fill out a short questionnaire on how they use and how they like our products. Make them a special offer on new or different merchandise (accessories, for example). These people are generally satisfied and loyal customers. They are valuable assets. Here's an opportunity to show them that we are a good company to do business with.

Both groups have agreed that improvements can be made right now in our repair and service division at moderate expense. Let's do it.

185

Sample Business Plan

This business plan is for the acquisition of the cutting machine division of the Allison Machine Company by the Proctor Manufacturing Company.

INTRODUCTION

The Proctor Manufacturing Company (PMC) was organized for the primary purpose of purchasing a single product line from the Allison Machine Company (AMC) of Chicago, Illinois. The product was a specialized type of reciprocating cutting machine that was invented and patented in 1922 and designed for use in the sign and display industries for cutting out complex and irregular shapes in sheet materials such as plywood, cardboard, and plastics. AMC bought the patents and manufactured the product in its large industrial tool and equipment division in Chicago.

The sales of the cutting machine grew to more than $170,000 annually and this unique machine was an important and profitable product for AMC until 1954 when changes in the sign and display industries reduced the need for this type of machine. Sales started to level off as early as 1952 and by 1958 they had declined to less than $100,000 per year.

Rather than try to develop new applications for the machine, AMC decided in 1960 to try to sell the cutting machine product line as a going business (it was still profitable) or, if this could not be done, to discontinue its manufacture.

A group of investors who owned a small manufacturing company in Connecticut (Precision Parts, Inc.) heard about the AMC cutting machine through another small manufacturing company. Precision Parts had a contract machining operation serving the aircraft industry and business was not very good in 1958. The owners decided to try to acquire another small company or product line that could supplement their dwindling contract business. Precision Parts thought that the AMC cutting machine would give them some good production runs for their milling machines and turret lathes, which were underutilized.

A trip to Chicago to talk to AMC and look at their operations convinced the sales manager of Precision that the cutting machine would be an ideal product line, not only because it would provide work for the machine shop but because they could sell the AMC cutting machine to many other industries where it was virtually unknown.

After a preliminary examination of the financial history and general prospectus provided by AMC and a meeting of the presidents of Precision Parts and Allison, Precision instructed its lawyers to form a new corporation for the purpose of acquiring and manufacturing new products. The Proctor Manufacturing Company was formed as a wholly owned subsidiary of Precision Parts, Inc. and serious negotiations were started with Allison. The business plan that follows was prepared in 1960 by the author, who was one of the owners of Precision Parts, Inc. Some editing has been done and names and figures have been disguised for the sake of privacy, but the essential elements of the plan are based on the acquisition, which was consummated in 1961. A copy of the purchase and sale agreement is attached as Appendix E-2. As of 1987 the cutting machine, which has been in continuous production for 64 years, is still being manufactured by Proctor with modifications and improvements. Thousands of these machines are in use today in a wide variety of interesting and valuable applications and, as indicated in the sales history, the largest sales volume ever achieved annually was in 1986.

As a sequel to this business plan and the purchase of the AMC cutting machine division by Proctor, the author, who is still associated with the company, has added a review of the operations since acquisition. He has also added a "hindsight" commentary.

Here is the business plan that was used by Proctor to get a $50,000 loan from a small local bank:

A PROPOSAL TO ACQUIRE CERTAIN ASSETS OF THE ALLISON MACHINE COMPANY BY THE PROCTOR MANUFACTURING COMPANY

Product Description

The AMC cutting machine operates on the principle of the sabre saw with several unique features:

1. The cutting head swivels 360° automatically in either direction.

2. The available cutting tools are not only wood and metal saw blades but chisels, knives (for cloth), step cutters (for plastic), and combination chisel and toothed blades.

3. The depth of cut is adjustable from less than $\frac{1}{32}''$ to over $2''$.

4. The stroke is adjustable.

5. The cutting speed is adjustable.

6. Shadow-free lighting of the pinch point is provided within the machine.

There are only three models available: the curved base plate type (for cutting curved die board), the flat base plate type (for general use), and the fixed stroke machine with rigid guide tube (for heavy duty). All models are offered with 115 volt or 220 volt AC motors. There are 23 different blades available from stock. The average life of the machine is about 20 years. Some are still operating after 40 years of use while others in severe and difficult applications wear out in 2 or 3 years. Complete repair and rebuilding service is maintained by the present manufacturer and spare parts are available for 10 years after a model is discontinued. All blades and some parts, common to all models regardless of age, are available through a well-established network of dealers in all major population areas in the United States and more than 25 foreign countries.

The basic price of the machine is $175.00 FOB factory. Repeat orders for expendable items such as blades, belts, and bulbs comprise 38% of the total sales. Dealers are allowed a 25% discount if they stock machines and supplies.

The Market

The AMC cutting machine was originally developed for the purpose of cutting out wood and cardboard letters, figures, and displays primarily for movie theaters and the sign industry. In the 1920s and 1930s fancy cut-out displays were used in virtually every movie theater in the United States and most of the machines were sold to theaters or to freelance display artists who did the cut out work for the movie houses.

Gradually this machine became popular with large department stores for making window displays in house. Marshall Field had 25 machines in constant use in its display department in the early 1930s.

In the 1940s the cutting machine was used as a template and pattern cutter in the aircraft industry. It also was used in boat building, lamp shade manufacturing, stencil making, the shoe industry, model building (especially topographic models), and several other specialized industries where the precise cutting of sheet materials was important. However, the dominant market was the neighborhood movie theater, which fell into steep decline during and after World War II. This decline triggered AMC's decision to sell or discontinue the product.

Future Markets

Precision Parts has had considerable experience with several industries where the AMC cutting machine would be valuable but for unknown reasons was never used or even tried out. These industries are:

1. The steel rule die industry, especially the rotary die segment of this industry, which is a relatively new concept in the conversion of corrugated board.

2. The infant but promising composite materials industry, which is now developing structural materials made of fiber glass, epoxied laminates, and so on.

3. The newly emerging franchised art and award market, which involves custom framing, matting, and logotypes of awards, certificates, scriptological items (old stock certificates and documents), numismatic and philatelic items.

These markets have been ignored by AMC. Our research indicates that 50 to 100 machines per year could be sold in these markets now.

Competition

There is virtually no competition in the United States or Canada. The AMC machine was protected for 17 years with several basic patents (all of which have expired) that allowed it to gain a very strong market position and thousands of satisfied and loyal customers. We have interviewed 20 customers in New England and are much impressed with their very favorable comments on the AMC machine.

The machine is extremely well designed and engineered. There are more than 200 individual parts in the machine, some of which are complex and unique. This complexity would probably deter any company that might consider copying the AMC design. However, in 1935 an English company copied the then-current model and was able to capture the entire European and British Commonwealth markets. Patent protection was limited to the United States and Canada.

A brand new, greatly improved model was introduced in

1938 and much of the European sales were recaptured. A recent investigation of the European market by AMC indicated that the British competitor is still selling about 100 units a year of the old copy of AMC's 1935 model. AMC stated that the British competitor is interested in selling out and this opportunity should be explored by Proctor.

Manufacturing

The present manufacturing facilities available to Proctor are well suited to make many of the more difficult AMC machined parts. The jigs, fixtures, and tooling can easily be adapted to Proctor's equipment. The only major machine required by Proctor would be a small surface grinder (cost about $4000 new, $1500 used).

The estimated space required for equipment, inventory, and assembly for the AMC cutting machine is about 3000 square feet. The space is already available in the east wing of the Precision building and can be made available to Proctor within one week. Assembly benches and storage shelving are available.

The increased work load required for the AMC machine could be completely handled by the existing machinery and personnel of Precision, with the addition of one surface grinder.

Good, up-to-date engineering and assembly drawings are available from AMC. If a contract is executed to purchase the assets from AMC, they have agreed to produce 100 complete machines in excess of normal sales with the Proctor name plate. This will allow ample time to close down the manufacturing operation in Chicago; ship the equipment, inventory, and records to Connecticut; and set up the new operation within 30 days with little or no interruption in customer service. The cost of the extra 100 machines will be AMC's factory cost and overhead plus 10%.

Cost Projections

Proctor has had three employees and the company auditors visit the AMC operation in Chicago. The Proctor foreman has spent several days with the foreman at AMC. AMC has other products going through the same manufacturing operations and it has been difficult to determine exact costs on the cutting machine. However, AMC factory overhead appears to be at least 25% higher than that of Proctor. This has been verified by Proctor accountants and it is reasonable to assume that manufacturing costs at Proctor will be somewhat lower than at AMC.

Another cost factor involves the purchase of cutting blades from an outside vendor. Proctor's engineer has suggested blade design changes that could dramatically lower blade costs. Preliminary discussions with suppliers and new design samples have confirmed this.

Proctor's management is confident that material and manufacturing costs can be reduced by a minimum of 10%.

Pricing

AMC has not had a price increase on the cutting machine in three years. It also has a very short discount policy for dealers that gives them little incentive to stock the machine or blades.

Proctor management feels that a 5% price increase can easily be introduced, especially if dealer discounts and deliveries were improved. It is the intention of Proctor to schedule a price increase within 6 months after acquiring the

AMC assets and allow dealers to buy at the old prices for 15 days after the new price announcement. Together with an improvement in the dealer discount and delivery, Proctor should show a gross margin of about 50% on sales for the initial 12 months of new ownership.

Customer Service

AMC's service to its customers for the cutting machines is terrible. Deliveries run anywhere from 30 to 60 days. The operating instructions on the machine are inadequate and poorly presented. Parts lists and service information are antiquated. Packaging is unimpressive.

In spite of all of these shortcomings the machine is superbly engineered, ruggedly built, highly reliable, easy to use, and well liked by everyone with whom we talked. Some of those interviewed have owned the same machine for 20 or 30 years.

Dealer Organization

AMC cutting machine dealers do not sell—they take orders. This is not surprising when you look at the meager discounts they get and the lack of marketing support from the manufacturer. Most factory communication with dealers is by phone or correspondence. Very seldom do they ever see a representative from the factory.

There are 22 active dealers at present covering the entire United States (except the Chicago area) and Canada. Of these dealers, 5 sell fewer than 10 machines per year.

The Chicago area (northern Illinois and southern Wisconsin) was handled out of the Chicago factory by a full-time salaried AMC salesman until his untimely death in

1958. No replacement was made. He sold approximately 300 machines per year. By comparison 70 machines per year are sold by the New York dealer and 35 per year by the Los Angeles dealer.

We estimate that the potential for sales in the New York area is around 300 per year and in Los Angeles about 200.

The AMC dealers frequently carried other nonrelated product lines of AMC and many of the dealers are not well suited to sell the cutting machine. We feel that the U.S. and Canadian markets justify at least 50 dealers and we believe it would not be difficult to secure them. Preliminary investigations tend to confirm this.

If we can be successful in penetrating markets where the machine is not now sold (die making, composite materials, graphic arts, and model making), we could justify 100 dealers and we believe this could be done within five years.

Dealers must be given better discounts and more factory support (application data sheets, good parts lists, periodic sales meetings, inquiry referrals from national advertising, etc.) as well as sales goals.

Advertising

AMC dropped their advertising budget in 1958 by 50% for the cutting machine. We believe that $6000 should be budgeted for advertising if Proctor buys the AMC assets.

A completely new catalog is necessary. This should be designed along with a 3 × 5 envelope stuffer for direct mail and dealer counter use. All literature, printed matter, letter heads, tags, and labels of Proctor should have a coordinated family resemblance. A new logo for Proctor will be developed.

Institutional advertising should be placed in the important trade papers serving the industries where the machine is now sold. Plans for ads in new market media should be prepared for use within 12 months after acquisition.

A survey of direct mail potential should be started as soon as practical, and mailing lists should be assembled for use in target industries when test marketing indicates that a potential exists.

Personnel

As indicated in the personnel requirements projected for this operation, no new personnel will be required during the first year. However, training will be required of those workers who will do the assembly, testing, and quality control. This will be the responsibility of the Precision factory manager.

The seller has agreed to have up to three employees from Proctor spend one week at the AMC factory in Chicago to become acquainted with the systems and procedures used by AMC in the manufacture of the cutting machine.

Precision sales personnel will have the responsibility for advertising and selling the cutting machine. A marketing plan has already been developed with the help of the AMC sales manager.

Accounting

A separate set of books are required for Proctor as this is a wholly owned subsidiary of Precision Parts, Inc. Intercompany transactions will be fully accounted for in the normal manner of manufacturer/supplier relations. Marketing and administrative service will be billed at a rate to be established by Precision management and the company auditors. Space will be allocated to the Proctor operation and billed at the rate of $3.00 per square foot per year.

It is estimated that 3000 square feet will be needed; thus the rent charge will be about $9000 per year (not shown in the pro forma projections shown in Appendix E-1).

Administration

Proctor will need administrative services from Precision such as order processing, payroll, accounting, and reporting. This will be provided by Precision.

All officers of Precision will be elected officers of Proctor and be responsible for these functions in both companies. The board of directors of Precision will also serve as directors of Proctor.

Financing

The asking price of AMC for all the assets associated with the cutting machine division is $125,000 with cash at closing.

Our pro forma estimates of profit are shown in Appendix E-1 at the following projected annual sales levels:

$119,109

$125,000

$150,000

The sales for 1960 are projected by AMC at $119,109 and it seems likely that this will be achieved. Although we are quite confident that we can increase sales and reduce costs, our projected return on investment should be based on a very modest increase in sales. The pro forma profit as shown with sales at $119,109 should be used to estimate return on investments. The profit projected of $20,179 for 1961 represents a 17% return before tax on an investment of

$85,000. It does not assume a significant increase in sales or reduction in costs nor does it allow for any unforeseen contingencies. However, the risk factor is extremely low.

A starting offer of $65,000 cash at closing is suggested. If we believe that the seller will negotiate, we should be prepared to negotiate up to $85,000 with some financing assumed by the seller. The return on investment in this situation would be over 20% and preferably 25%.

If the seller will not go below $95,000, additional concessions can be requested, such as inventory over one year's supply will be paid for at the beginning of the year used, any inventory not used within two years to be paid for at one-half the inventory cost at the end of the second year, and help in financing.

If a deal can be made between $75,000 and $95,000, Precision Parts, Inc. will be able to contribute $25,000 in the form of equity capital in the wholly owned subsidiary, Proctor Manufacturing Company, Inc. A bank loan will be needed for the balance, and all of the assets of Proctor will be available to secure the loan. Precision can guarantee the loan if required.

Discussions with the bank should begin immediately. If bank rates and terms are not acceptable, each of the four stockholders of Precision will be asked to loan Proctor $15,000 to $20,000.

Expectations

The pro forma profit and loss projections for Proctor are very conservative and will almost certainly be exceeded even if unanticipated problems arise.

It is quite obvious that the Allison Manufacturing Company has completely lost interest in the cutting machine product line and has not put any effort or money into this operation in several years. AMC has been eminently successful in other product areas with profitable sales of over $20 million in 1959. The cutting machine line with less than $100,000 sales in 1958 has no impact whatsoever on their other operations. However, they have expressed concern that closing down the cutting machine operation would create ill will, which they would prefer to avoid. They are anxious to sell this product line, but they want assurance that the buyer has the capability to serve the customers well.

Proctor is ideally suited to protect and enhance the AMC reputation and this advantage is being emphasized during negotiations with AMC.

If sales of $200,000 per year can be achieved by 1966 (and we believe they can be), this will have been a very successful acquistion for Precision and will enable us to start looking for another acquisition within a short time.

WHAT HAPPENED?

Usually in text book cases the outcome is never revealed or it is fictionalized and does not serve well as a learning experience. In the real case of the sale and purchase of the AMC cutting machine by the Proctor Manufacturing Company, there is a fully documented sequel.

On May 23, 1961, Allison Machine Company and the Proctor Manufacturing Company signed the agreement shown in Exhibit E-2. As indicated, the purchase price was less than $85,000 due to rather aggressive negotiating on the part of Proctor.

AMC built the 100 machines requested by Proctor and all were shipped to Connecticut with the inventory. Due to the large and complex operations of AMC, some inventory not belonging to the cutting machine was also shipped. This error caused some confusion and difficulty but was amicably settled in due time. The relationship between Proctor and AMC was very cordial during negotiations and the transfer of assets. On several occasions Proctor called upon AMC for help and advice, which was given promptly and courteously. All cutting machine orders and customer inquiries that were received by AMC after the closing were forwarded to Proctor, often with helpful notes.

Three of Proctor's employees spent a week at the AMC plant in Chicago and had an enriching experience in meeting their counterpart employees at AMC and learning about the cutting machine. Many Precision employees were involved in the Proctor acquisition and the team effort served to keep morale and productivity at a high level.

All literature, owner manual, and parts lists were completely revised with new graphics, exploded drawings, and "user friendly" copy.

During the five years after the acquisition, Proctor established 21 new dealers and several new applications were developed for the cutting machine. In 1963 an order was received from the U.S. Government for 100 machines, the largest order ever received in the product's history.

Sales before and after acquisition have been as follows (these figures do not include parts and repairs):

Year	Units	Dollars	Year	Units	Dollars	Year	Units	Dollars
1951	769	172,804	1963	587	134,271	1975	698	234,524
1952	741	169,478	1964	561	146,961	1976	811	281,169
1953	747	170,603	1965	754	170,126	1977	735	284,640
1954	707	164,967	1966	786	172,246	1978	834	350,276
1955	738	161,516	1967	773	180,516	1979	744	353,244
1956	674	142,162	1968	785	197,673	1980	633	345,451
1957	486	101,455	1969	842	214,963	1981	645	389,392
1958	468	97,683	1970	631	184,276	1982	553	352,647
1959	481	105,945	1971	763	210,466	1983	495	333,791
1960	474	102,671	1972	827	234,835	1984	686	478,149
1961	515	109,758	1973	763	234,944	1985	645	459,595
1962	533	113,516	1974	868	259,254	1986	895	597,012

Cost reductions were achieved on many of the component parts. Some parts, however, suffered serious cost increases and the overall reduction in costs so confidently predicted in the business plan did not materialize. Nevertheless, the profit goals were met and the Proctor Manufacturing Company contributed significantly to the earnings of its parent.

The cutting machine is still owned (in 1987) by Proctor and was the second of five small manufacturing companies or product lines acquired by Precision during a 20-year period.

As can be seen from the record of unit sales, there was a general improvement and although inflation accounted for much of the dollar increase, Proctor showed a good profit every year since its acquisition. The overall return on investment has been superior.

The cutting machine is now 65 years old (with continued improvements in design and function) and still retains its unique characteristics. There are thousands of units in daily use by satisfied and loyal customers throughout the United States and 33 foreign countries.

This acquisition is an excellent example of the benefits of buying and selling product lines among small manufacturing companies. The sale has benefited not only the buyer but the seller, who was pleased to sell the product line at the negotiated price. However, there are many other benefits that came out of this transaction:

1. Not a single person was deprived of a job. As a matter of fact, both the buyer and seller ultimately hired more people as a result of this sale.

2. Surplus space, personnel, and machinery were fully utilized in the most productive manner.

3. Thousands of AMC machine owners were assured of a reliable and continuous source of service, parts, and new machines.

4. New applications of the machine were successfully developed by the buyer as the old applications gradually disappeared.

5. The success of the acquisition was an important factor in enabling Precision Parts to acquire four other small companies and product lines over the next 20 years and grow from $300,000 to over $8,000,000 in annual sales and from 12 to 80 employees.

6. Precision now has a payroll and benefit program in excess of $2 million per year and spends more than $2 million annually for goods and services in Connecticut.

APPENDIX E-1: PRO FORMA INCOME AND EXPENSE

Sales[a]	119,109	125,000	150,000
Material (38%)	45,720	47,500	57,000
Direct labor and subcontract (16%)	19,000	20,000	24,000
Gross profit	54,389	57,500	69,000
Amortization of tooling (35,000/5 yrs.)	7,000	7,000	7,000
	47,389	50,500	62,000
Other direct costs			
Depreciation on new equipment (2000/5 years)	400	400	400
Tools maintenance	1,200	1,200	1,200
Acquisition costs	2,000	2,000	2,000
Shipping supplies	700	750	800
Insurance	1,100	1,100	1,100
Payroll taxes	530	530	530
Property taxes	1,280	1,280	1,280
	7,210	7,260	7,310
Administrative and selling expenses			
Manager	7,500	7,500	8,500
Secretary	3,600	3,600	4,200
Telephone	400	450	500
Office supplies	500	550	600
Professional	200	250	300
Payroll taxes	300	300	350
Advertising and literature	6,000	6,000	6,000
Travel and entertainment	1,000	1,000	1,000
Postage and sundry	500	600	700
	20,000	20,500	29,960
Net income before tax and parent charges	20,179	22,740	34,730

[a]Sales are about 61% units, 39% blades and parts.
NOTE: Tooling, new equipment, depreciation, and acquisition costs of $9,400 disappear after 5 years.

APPENDIX E-2: PURCHASE AGREEMENT

This agreement, dated May 23, 1961, between the Allison Machine Company, an Illinois Corporation, having its principal offices at 342 Monroe Street, Chicago, Illinois (hereinafter referred to as the "Seller") and the Proctor Manufacturing Company, a Connecticut Corporation, having its principal offices in the town of Bethel, Connecticut (hereinafter referred to as the "Purchaser").

Witnesseth:

Whereas, the Seller has been engaged for many years in the business, among others, of manufacturing, selling and distributing a cutting machine for cutting sheet materials and its related accessories and desires to sell such business and discontinue the same, and

Whereas, the Purchaser desires to acquire said business by purchase and engage therein;

Now, therefore it is mutually agreed as follows:

1. The Seller represents, warrants, and agrees to and with the purchaser, as follows:

   (a) Seller is a corporation duly organized and validly existing in good standing under the laws of the State of Illinois, and has full corporate power to make this agreement and carry out its terms. All corporate action on the part of its directors and shareholders necessary to make this agreement a valid legally binding contract enforceable in accordance with its terms has been taken.

   (b) Seller has delivered to Purchaser a statement of profit and loss relating to its cutting machine business for the period from 8/1/54 to 4/30/61 on a fiscal year basis, a copy of which statement is annexed hereto as Schedule A. Such statement truly and correctly reflects the net sales, flat labor and material costs, and gross profit realized by Seller from its cutting machine operations and business for the periods indicated; and there has been no materially substantial adverse change in such sales, flat labor and material costs, or gross profit since the last date reflected therein.

(c) Seller has delivered to Purchaser its cutting machine price list designated Form A-43, effective March 2, 1959, which is the current price list of Seller and truly and correctly reflects the prevailing prices and data relating to new and factory rebuilt cutting machines, accessories, and cutting blades. A copy of such price list is annexed hereto as Schedule B.

(d) Seller has delivered to Purchaser its cost sheets relating to the component parts of the cutting machines as follows:

Pages numbered 1 through 4 inclusive dated 4/27/59

Page 5 dated 8/22/59 and redated 12/22/59

Page 6 dated 11/12/59 and redated 12/22/59

A copy of each of such cost sheets is annexed hereto as Schedule C. Such cost sheets completely and correctly reflect the quantity, part number, description, material cost and direct labor cost of all component parts of the cutting machine as stated therein and together completely and correctly reflect such data for the aggregate assembled cutting machine including its standard equipment and packing material (domestic and export) both with and without carrying case.

(e) Seller has delivered to Purchaser a list (11 pages) dated 2/23/61 of major items of tooling (other than machinery) required and used in the manufacture, repair, and assembly of the cutting machine, indicating a total cost of such tooling in excess of forty two thousand eight hundred ($42,800.00) dollars, which list is true and correct to the best of Seller's knowledge and belief. Prior to the closing date and simultaneous with the delivery of the merchandise, materials and supply inventories as hereinafter provided, Seller shall deliver to Purchaser a complete and accurate list of such tooling, represented and warranted to be true and correct, to be transferred and sold to Purchaser hereunder stating for each item the part numbers operation number, tool number, description, and location of such item, if not in Seller's possession to be physically delivered to Purchaser.

(f) Seller has delivered to Purchaser a list of cutting machine dealers in the United States and Canada, which list is complete and correct. On the closing date Seller shall deliver to Purchaser a new list of such dealers and other customers of Seller corrected to reflect all changes in such list up to the closing date and to include all omissions therefrom, if any, which list shall be represented and warranted to be correct and complete.

(g) All contracts and arrangements with dealers and other customers of Seller are subject to cancellation by Seller without liability upon not more than thirty (30) days notice.

(h) There are no purchase commitments with suppliers or sales commitments with customers relating to the cutting machine business other than those made in the ordinary course of business.

(i) Seller has the sole and exclusive right to the use of the trademark and trade name of the cutting machine, which has been duly registered and is maintained current and in good standing both in the United States and Canada; and Seller has the unrestricted right to transfer and assign such trademark and trade name to Purchaser.

(j) Seller has not licensed or franchised any other person, firm, or corporation to manufacture, sell, or distribute the cutting machine or its parts or accessories, except for its own supply and purchase.

(k) Seller is the owner, having good and marketable title to all of the tangible and intangible properties, assets, rights, franchises, and contracts to be sold, transferred, conveyed, and assigned to Purchaser hereunder, which together represent all of the assets relating to its cutting machine business, except as herein excluded, free and clear of all claims, encumbrances, liens and charges.

(l) All inventories of tangible personal property to be sold and delivered hereunder to Purchaser consist of items of the quality and quantity usable or saleable in the normal and regular course of the cutting machine business of Seller, and all obsolete items and items below standard quality have been discarded or eliminated. All such items of inventory conform to Seller's prints and specifications therefor.

(m) To the best of Seller's knowledge, information, and belief, all patents relating to the cutting machine and its accessories have expired and the

same may be manufactured, assembled, distributed, and sold without infringement of any existing patents. No claims of any patent infringement
have been made or threatened against the Seller.

(n) Seller has paid the sales and/or use tax on all items
of tangible personal property to be sold hereunder, which are subject to such tax in its hands
under applicable Illinois statutes.

2. Subject to the representations and warranties herein
contained and to the terms, conditions, and provisions of
this agreement, the Seller agrees to sell, assign, and transfer
to Purchaser, and the Purchaser agrees to buy from the
Seller on the closing date as hereinafter fixed, all of Seller's
right, title, and interest in and to the properties, rights,
franchises, contracts, and assets of Seller's cutting machine
business, more particularly described as follows:

(a) All raw materials, finished and unfinished goods,
parts, and supplies required for and relating to the
manufacture, production, assembly, and fabrica-
tion of the cutting machine complete with standard equipment, and its accessories, including
cutting blades, all as set forth and offered by Seller
in its price list A-41, which is hereto annexed as
Schedule B, and all boxes, cartons, and other con-
tainers used for packing and shipping the above
described inventory. All such items of inventory
shall be set forth on a schedule thereof prepared
by Seller and to be delivered to Purchaser on June
22, 1961. Purchaser shall be permitted full opportunity to check and verify said inventory schedule prior to closing date. Such inventory schedule
shall set forth the quantity, part number, description, unit price determined as set forth below, the

total aggregate price for each item and for the entire inventory. The unit price for each item of inventory shall be determined as follows:

(i) For all items listed in Seller's cost sheets Schedule C annexed hereto, the stated cost of the material relating to the cutting machine plus two hundred (200%) percent of the direct labor, if any, as indicated thereon.

(ii) All other items at Seller's cost, for which Seller shall furnish to Purchaser supporting cost records to substantiate.

Anything herein contained to the contrary notwithstanding, Purchaser shall not be required to purchase (i) any greater quantity of any item than that necessary for the production of one thousand (1000) cutting machines, complete with standard equipment as described in said price list A-41, Schedule 13 hereto annexed; (ii) any greater quantity of any item for the production of all accessories for the cutting machine listed on said price list A-41 than twice the amount thereof sold by Seller during any twelve consecutive months since August 1, 1959; (iii) a total of all items hereunder in excess of forty-five thousand ($45,000.00) dollars in the aggregate; nor (iv) any item of inventory that bears the name of Seller inserted, printed, or affixed thereto in such fashion as to not be readily removable without marring or damaging such item. In addition, Purchaser shall have the right to purchase from time to time prior to the expiration of one (1) year after the closing date, from Seller's retained inventory, parts, and accessories for other models of the cutting machine at reasonable prices to be determined by Seller, as well as such portion of the cutting machine inventory of Seller to be sold hereunder as may be in excess of forty-five thousand ($45,000) dollars, at the same prices stated herein.

(b) All special tools required for the manufacture, production, assembly, repair, inspection, and testing of the cutting machine, its parts, accessories
and standard equipment, including, without limitation special dies, fixtures, jigs, gauges, bars,
plates, form tools, cams, cutters, vices, and drills.
As required by paragraph 1(e) above, Seller shall
deliver to Purchaser on June 22, 1961, a schedule
of such tooling to be sold hereunder to Purchaser,
and Purchaser shall be permitted full opportunity
to check and verify the same prior to the closing
date. There is excluded from this agreement and
purchase, all machinery and all general-purpose
machine tools and equipment for the manufacture
of the cutting machine as set forth in the list dated
October 14, 1960, furnished to the Purchaser by
Seller by letter of transmittal dated February 17,
1961.

(c) All prints, drawings, tracings, process sheets,
bills of materials, specifications, line ups, standard operation sheets, time study records, and all
other records, data, and information relating to,
used in, or useful for the production, assembly,
maintenance, repair, sale, and distribution of the
cutting machine, its accessories, and equipment,
including cutting blades, together with all business records since August 1, 1957, pertaining-
thereto, including a list of all dealers and direct
customers, correspondence, invoices, statistics,
and accounts pertaining to purchasing, selling, advertising, distribution, and promotion
of the cutting machine business. Sales literature,
artwork, photos, plates, and related materials
shall be included to the extent the same are

in the possession of or under control of the Seller. Purchaser agrees that it will retain all of said papers, instruments, and documents turned over to it for a period of not less than five (5) years after the closing date; and Seller shall have an opportunity at any time and from time to time during reasonable business hours to examine said papers, instruments, and documents.

(d) All U.S. and foreign patents, if any, trademarks and trade names, including registrations therefor, copyrights and applications therefor, if any, relating to the cutting machine and its accessories.

(e) The exclusive right to trademarks, trade names, and the good will of said cutting machine business.

(f) All contracts with dealers and other customers, copies of which shall be delivered to Purchaser prior to the closing date for Purchaser's inspection and Purchaser agrees to assume the performance of such contracts and to indemnify Seller from any liability in connection therewith.

(g) Any purchase commitments made in the ordinary course of business for materials, parts, or supplies relating to the cutting machine and its accessories shall be described and set forth in full by Seller in a schedule to be delivered to Purchaser, and Purchaser shall have the right to review such commitments and assume the performance of only such as Purchaser may deem advisable in connection with the agreement, and Purchaser agrees to indemnify Seller from any liability in connection therewith.

3. The purchase price shall be an amount equal to the aggregate of the following:

(a) For the tangible personal property to be sold to Purchaser under paragraph 2(a) above, and which is fully described and itemized in the schedule provided for thereunder, such sum as shall be determined by application of the pricing formula set forth in said paragraph 2(a) but not in excess of forty-five thousand ($45,000) dollars, it being understood and agreed that items of inventory in excess of such amount shall be deleted from such inventory at the selection of Purchaser.

(b) For the tangible personal property to be sold to Purchaser under paragraphs 2(b) and 2(c), the sum of thirty-two thousand five hundred ($32,500) dollars.

(c) For the tangible and intangible personal property, acontracts, rights, and other assets to be sold to Purchaser under paragraphs 2(d), (e), (f), and (g), and all other rights, franchises, agreements, and assets to be sold and transferred to Purchaser hereunder the sum of one ($1.00) dollar.

Such purchase price shall be paid to Seller (i) seven thousand ($7,000.00) dollars upon the signing and delivery of this agreement, and (ii) the balance on the closing date as hereinafter fixed upon fulfillment of and compliance with the terms and conditions of this agreement to be performed at or prior to the closing date. Payment shall be made in cash, or by certified or bank cashier's check for such balance of the purchase price.

4. The closing date shall be June 30, 1961, at 10:00 AM

Chicago time at the offices of the Seller, or at such other date, time, and place as shall be mutually agreed upon between the parties. At the closing Seller shall deliver to Purchaser possession and title of all the properties, rights, and assets to be sold hereunder. All deeds, assignments, bills of sale, and other documents of transfer and title necessary for such purpose shall be duly executed and acknowledged by Seller and shall be prepared by Seller at its sole cost and expense for delivery to Purchaser on the closing date.

5. Seller covenants and agrees that it will not engage, and it will not knowingly permit, any of its officers, directors, or employees while under its control to engage for a period of five (5) years from the closing date, directly or indirectly, either as principal agent, officer, employee, stockholder, or otherwise, in manufacturing, repairing, selling, distributing, or any other phase of the cutting machine business or that of a similar tool or device, anywhere in the United States, Canada, or elsewhere where customers of the cutting machine may be.

6. Seller further warrants and agrees:

   (a) Pending the closing hereunder, Purchaser shall have full access to Seller's premises and to the books and records of Seller relating to its cutting machine business, and Seller's officers will furnish Purchaser with such financial and operating data and other information relating to such cutting machine business as Purchaser may from time to time reasonably request.

   (b) Pending the closing hereunder, Seller will conduct its cutting machine business only in the ordinary and usual course and manner, including without limitation, the maintenance of regular trade relations and practices with dealers, customers, and suppliers, and standard sales and pricing policies, methods, and practices.

(c) Seller has not, and Purchaser represents and warrants that it has not, retained any broker nor agreed to pay any fee or commission to any agent, broker, or finder for or on account of this agreement or the purchase contemplated hereby.

(d) Seller will indemnify and hold the Purchaser harmless from all debts, claims, demands, losses, liabilities, and expenses that may be asserted by creditors of Seller pursuant to the Illinois Bulk Sales Act.

(e) Seller will indemnify and hold the Purchaser harmless from all claims that may be asserted as a result of personal injury caused by said cutting machine manufactured and sold by the Seller prior to the closing date.

(f) All representations and warranties under this agreement or as provided herein shall survive the closing hereunder and any investigation at any time made by the Purchaser.

(g) Seller will execute and deliver, or cause to be executed and delivered, such additional instruments of title or transfer as Purchaser may require and request for the purpose of carrying out this agreement.

7. Purchaser's obligations to purchase and pay for the properties, rights, contracts, and assets of said cutting machine business shall be subject (a) to the satisfaction, on or prior to the closing date, of the accuracy of and compliance with the representations, warranties, and agreements of Seller contained herein, (b) to the performance by Seller

of its agreements set forth herein, and (c) the condition that such representations and warranties shall be deemed to have been made again and as of the time of closing and shall then be true in all material respects, as to which Seller shall deliver its certificate duly executed by an officer certifying in such detail as Purchaser may reasonably request as to the fulfillment of the above conditions.

8. In order to facilitate the transfer of title and possession of the properties and assets to be sold hereunder to Purchaser, and assist the Purchaser in transporting to and establishing the cutting machine business in Bethel, Connecticut, Seller agrees, during the period from June 22, 1961, when the inventory schedules under paragraphs 2(a) and 2(b) are to be delivered to Purchaser, and the closing date, to cooperate fully with Purchaser's representatives in checking and verifying such inventories and in packaging and packing the same for shipment to Purchaser's place of business. Purchaser and Seller will use their respective best efforts to expedite such checking, verification, and preparation for shipment so that as soon as the same is completed the closing date may be fixed prior to June 30, 1961, is feasible. Seller shall be reimbursed for any reasonable out-of-pocket expenses it may incur at the request of Purchaser in assisting in the packing and shipment of the properties and assets to be purchased hereunder. Seller further agrees to supply Purchaser after the closing date with any information and data as to the cutting machine business that Purchaser may reasonably request from time to time, and to forward to Purchaser, promptly upon receipt, all letters, inquiries, orders, and other communications relating to the cutting machine business received by Seller from suppliers, dealers, customers, and others.

9. This agreement shall be binding upon and enforceable by the parties hereto and their respective successors and assigns.

10. This agreement may be amended only in writing signed by the parties or their successors and assigns, and may be executed in one or more counterparts, all which taken together shall constitute one instrument.

In witness whereof, the parties hereto have caused this agreement to be duly executed and their respective seals affixed the day and year first above written.

Allison Machine Company, Inc.

by _____

attest _____

Proctor Manufacturing Company, Inc.

by _____

attest _____

(b) 20. This Agreement may be executed by any facsimile, and shall be binding to the parties to their successors and assigns, and may be executed in one or more counterparts, all which taken together shall constitute one instrument.

In witness whereof, the parties hereto have caused this Agreement to be fully executed and their respective seals affixed, the individual above written.

ABC Machine Company, Inc.

By _____

_____
title

Factory Manufacturing Company

By _____

_____
title

Index